COSMIC KEYS TO MANIFESTATION

THE SEER SETS THE SEEN

I0310377

A NEW TRANSLATION AND COMMENTARY OF

Dṛg Dṛśya Viveka

THE SEER SETS THE SEEN

Cosmic Keys to Manifestation

A new translation and commentary of

दृग् दृश्य वविक

Dṛg Dṛśya Viveka

Attributed to: *Ādi Śaṅkarācārya*

The source text has been attributed to *Ādi Śaṅkarācārya* in the tradition of *Advaita Vedānta*. The name of *Śaṅkarā* is used as a placeholder by scholars and admirers from this preeminent school of non-duality. *Dṛg Dṛśya Viveka* was probably written by *Bhārati Tirtha* in the early 14th century.

Reverence to the Great Ones who assemble and continuously transmit this knowledge that we may experience harmony and disharmony at once.

Eternally unfolding appreciation to Jacqui for her edits to the book and to my personality.

"Butterfly Woman" artwork on front cover: Jordan Lucky
With thanks to Luke Davis and Goldbergs Coffee House
Book design: Brayden Maybury
Photograph on back cover: Dean Abraham

Published by Gorakhnath Pty Ltd

www.joshpryor.com.au
ISBN (Print): 978-0-6451211-4-8

Acknowledgement of Gender Privilege

Listen up everyone, a man is about to explain some lessons. This is a translation and commentary of an excellent text, written long ago by a man of unknown virtue, guarded and transcribed by male scholars, and translated with self-bestowed licence by a white Australian who has assumed the authority to do so. It's fine, this is a free country and we are lucky to have resources to do such things.

Far less excusable is the enduring legacy of patriarchy upon which all men, including the author, continue to profit. Women around the world face an immense array of burdens, those recognised and hidden, some undoubtedly heavier than others. Experiences range from violent damage to the body and psyche, to conditioning that begins in infancy, and the multitude of undercurrents against which they must swim for their entire lives. The process of unearthing and subverting this conditioning can be exhausting, especially for the pioneers in their countries, families, and workplaces. Strong-minded women undergo resistance, rejection, ridicule, re-education. A constant struggle that creates resilience in women which is often never required of men.

The ignorance of men regarding their privilege creates more disharmony. I consider myself to be a progressive masculine example, but I rarely come close to understanding the internal experience of being a woman in any culture. Meanwhile, every woman I have ever known has been conditioned to empathise and identify with my perspective.

Though built upon eons of patriarchy and wilful ignorance, may this book in some way reflect the courage you have shown.

Preface

I love yoga so much – and all of India's ancient sciences. Physical yoga is a marvel that induces the state we are looking for without reading anything. Just poses and breathing, resulting in health and vitality. For those with the time and inclination to go further there are thousands of modern books on yogic philosophy. For me, as a zealot of mysticism from way back, it was always going to involve the palm leaf verses. These compact Sanskrit texts induce the state we are looking for as well. When stacked upon the steady foundation of a daily practice of *āsana* and *prāṇāyāma*, acceleration is profound.

There are many other tools in history that have helped humanity know and embrace the metaphysical, mystical, psychic world. The really good ones don't spend too much time making sense of it, it's more important to use it. In this text there is a clear assessment of the human intellect, its nature and limitations. The intellect would have us settle for a "reasonable" explanation based on scraps of material evidence that our instruments and funding provide. Extraordinary claims require extraordinary evidence, as they say. Contrary to the principles of pure science, the intellect is far more comfortable resting on the assumption of limited material existence than exploring the mystical side.

But we want to learn and we want to give it a go. We will make sense of it the more we use it. This life is unique and precious, don't wait for corporate science to give you permission to do what the Great Ones wrote down thousands of years ago. Don't fall for the trick of thinking about that guy who was into spirituality and went crazy. People be acting crazy fairly often. After all, how many good citizens lose their marbles while following the prescribed life, in spite of modern medicine's accomplishments?

Humanity is a long lineage of enthusiastic people focused on acknowledging and studying the wider scope of life. Our species is built upon this desire to experience things on the edge of the tangible. We want to understand why that thought came at just the right time, why that other person knows so much about the future, why we wake up from sleep with the uncanny memory of something real and significant outside the scope of this human form.

The New Thought and Positive Psychology movements of the 19th and 20th centuries provide excellent entry points for people to directly enquire into their own nature. Scant on dogma, these authors took it upon themselves to validate their direct experience. This boldness is responsible for a lot of contact made with higher consciousness in subsequent decades.

When I was 20, visiting America, I left my friends at the hostel and went walking in the suburbs of San Francisco. Noticing a second-hand spiritualist bookshop, I approached. I entered and stood in the doorway. My eyes pointed at the bottom shelf of one of the racks. An unmarked blue hardcover book. I picked it up without looking at anything else, paid for it, and walked out.

It is not a well-known book or famous author, but it became a cornerstone of my practice. It belongs to the cultural transformation of the late 19th century and early 20th century, when prominent *yogi*-s travelled by boat to the West and mystical teachings from the East found a willing audience. In the decades to follow, white Americans published books on positive thinking and manifestation, with enough Christian flavour to make them publishable.

In years to come this theme would weave itself through my life via business-oriented self-development organisations that tapped into some of the key books of the era. Business development is rather unromantic and unspiritual on the surface, but this reflects the occult nuance of the teachings. They are in plain sight, yet unnoticed.

Nothing is ever truly hidden from us – we hide from ourselves. The external world is a mirror of the internal, so when we define teachings as occult or when we declare a part of our minds as "subconscious", they recede in-kind. Yoga and all the great teachings are simply a path to revealing ourselves again. Gradually, the intense vulnerability and humiliation of separation does indeed transform to ecstatic excitement, passion, and bliss.

Behaviours that would have been labelled kooky not too long ago are now addressed in modern books on "manifestation". The Law of Attraction material from recent decades is popular because it works, *at least some of the time*. What is needed to close the gap? Why does it work only sometimes? Why are certain people born with such staggering abilities? Why can't they replicate it on demand or produce outcomes society deems valuable?

Yoga and the ancient non-dual metaphysics of India brought things closer for me. Every experience I ever had or observed fits within this corpus, the threshold for entry is just a little steep. As I exposed myself to the very oldest texts I could find, sidestepping most modern commentaries and the *classical literature* approach to the language of Sanskrit, I found reliable contact in increasing measure.

The work you are about to read expounds upon a 14th century Sanskrit text called *Dṛg Dṛśya Viveka*. The title could be translated as "On the Nature of the Subject and its Objects". It comes from a different continent, tradition, and era of humankind compared to that book I gravitated toward in San Francisco, 25 years ago. Yet, it precisely echoes the structure of consciousness and mechanism of manifestation.

Everyone is alive, and you can liaise with them through their work. This activity widens your personal stance. Everything happens first in consciousness, and the subsequent manifestation from imagination is something you can take for granted. Let us appreciate and honour the reality of this very large present moment, swelling with options.

We can afford to put aside the scepticism for a little while. Don't worry, it can be picked up again any time. For now, we should honour our personal experience. Weird and wild things happen in consciousness, and ignorance of that reality is the only thing holding us back.

This colonial capitalist environment really is a toddler in the span of history. Look to the Greats for advice. When we stop spamming our mind and polluting our ocean, we will access the greater mind and the cosmic ocean, becoming who and what we intend.

१

Section One

Śloka 1—19

Refresher on Materialism

As far as we have come as a species, humanity still lumbers under the illusion of a temporary existence, separate from the whole, and the scarcity-victimhood dynamic this brings. Whether identifying as an atheist or a spiritual person, the default assumption is frequently the same:

> "I am a small person within a world much larger than me, and I must work with many forces, seen and unseen, along with the whims of other people, all of us living in a place we all call the external world."

Thousands of years of Vedic knowledge along with quantum physics and all manner of psychedelic experiences point to our ability to access a unified substrate of potential, from which classical physics and linear time emerge. But we still behave as though this human form is tiny and isolated, vulnerable to vast external threats and opportunities, when we could work directly with that substrate.

We tend to operate under the paradigm of materialism which asserts that: "Physical matter is the most fundamental thing."

It is an understandable point of view that comes directly from our sensory experience of the world. It definitely seems like physical things are the most real! There are literal building blocks from which we create houses, tools, and food, so it makes sense to construct a view of reality in the same way.

But it **only** makes sense from the sensory perspective. When we consider unseen forces, it all falls apart. It turns out the most fundamental substance, from which the physical springs forth is something else.

The first few *śloka* of *Dṛg Dṛśya Viveka* uses methodological reductionism, just like our own scientists do, to arrive at an answer to the question:

"What is most fundamental thing?"

The Most Fundamental Thing

Śloka 1 — 5

रूपं दृश्यं लोचनं दृक् तद्दृश्यमं दृक्तु मानसम्
दृश्या धीवृत्तयः साक्शी दृगेव न तु दृश्यते

rūpaṃ dṛśyaṃ locanaṃ dṛk tadṛśyamaṃ dṛktu mānasam
dṛśyā dhīvṛttayaḥ sākśī dṛgeva na tu dṛśyate

नीलपीतस्थूलसूक्श्म ह्रस्वदीर्घादिभेदतः
नानाविधानि रूपानि पश्येल्लोचनमेकधा

nīla-pīta-sthūla-sūkśma hrasva-dīrghādi-bhedataḥ
nānā-vidhāni rūpāni paśyel locanam ekadhā

आन्ध्यमान्द्यपतुत्वेषु नेत्रधर्मेषु चैकधा
संकल्पयेन्मनः श्रोत्र त्वगादौ योज्यतांइदम्

āndhya-māndya-patutveṣu netra-dharmeṣu caikadhā
saṃkalpayen manaḥ śrotr tvag-ādau yojyatāṃ idam

कामः संकल्पसन्देहौ श्रद्धाऽश्रद्धे धृतीतरे
ह्रीर्धीर्भीरित्येवमादीन् भासयत्येकधा चितिः

kāmaḥ saṃkalpa-sandehau śraddhā 'śraddhe dhṛtītare
hrīr dhīr bhīr ityevam ādīn bhāsayaty ekadhā citiḥ

नोदेति नास्तमेत्येषा न वृद्धिं याति न क्ष्यम्
स्वयं विभात्यथानन्यानि भासयेत् साधनं विना

nodeti nāstam ety eṣā na vṛddhiṃ yāti na kṣyam
svayaṃ vibhāty athānanyāni bhāsayet sādhanaṃ vinā

When we extrapolate from perceived physical forms to the eye organ, then to the mind, then to the perceiver of the mind, we find that the perceiver is the only thing not witnessed by another.

Physical forms have attributes and qualities, and this allows for the appearance of a diverse world of objects and a detailed material reality. These are perceived by the eye and the other sense organs.

Furthermore, the eye organ itself has attributes, and they are perceived by the mind. It is the same for the skin and other sense organs.

Extrapolating again, we find that states of the mind such as desire and doubt, beliefs and assumptions, moods, perceptions, opinions etc are all seen by a supervising luminosity.

The luminous perceiver, which this text calls *sākśī*, the Seer, does not change. It always exists and is not witnessed by another. Material objects, the skeleton, sense organs, and the physical mind are impermanent and subject to decay.

The Seer is permanent, and is thus most fundamental.

Why this different result from the ancient *rishi-s* compared to Western scientists and philosophers? Simply, the Westerners make an additional assumption before asking the question. They slide in a presupposition and they never look back. The question becomes:

> "Assuming that the world I see with my sense organs
> is outside of me, what is the most fundamental thing?"

If you ask the root question, *sans*-assumption, you get a solid answer. Assumptions are fine in principle, but this one is not required and it ought to be declared and pondered more often.

The next *śloka* rounds off the discovery and provides a useful tip.

Description of Ego/Intellect

Śloka 6—7

चिच्छाया वेशतो बुद्धौ भानं धीस्तु द्विधा स्थिता
एकाहंकृतिरन्या स्याद् अन्तः करणरूपिनी

cicchāyā 'veśato budau bhānaṃ dhīs tu dvidhā sthitā
ekāhaṃkṛtir anyā syād antaḥ-karaṇa-rūpinī

छायाहंकारयोरैक्यं तप्तायः पिण्डवन्मतम्
तदहंकारतादात्म्याद् देहश्चेतनतामगात्

chāyāhaṃkārayor aikyaṃ taptāyaḥ piṇḍavan matam
tad-ahaṃkāra-tādātmyād dehaś cetanatām agāt

THE SELF-CONTAINED SYSTEM of senses, moods, and mentality is represented using the words *buddhi*, mind, ego, and intellect.[1] This personality consists of self-image and beliefs. It is autonomous when running, yet it is completely dependent on the luminosity of the Seer. Wise ones note that as the personality (mind, ego) observes itself to be a remarkable and unique entity, it becomes vulnerable to the assumption that it also created the powering luminosity within.

○

Wise indeed to remember the points raised above. The ego consists of emotions, perceptions, thoughts, and beliefs. It is a logical and defined being, able to discern and act in the physical world. It has authority but is also **completely dependent** on something else for its power. An interesting situation as it feels self-responsible, but not self-sufficient. It grapples with insecurity, finding itself dependent on something it does not understand. It is from here that neuroticism appears, the struggle of that *buddhi* to cope with its self-perceived vulnerability.

---

[1] The terms *buddhi*, ego, intellect are used interchangeably throughout this book. It has also been referred to as the "objective mind". Some schools of Indian thought use the word *buddhi* differently, indicating a higher supreme intelligence. This sort of definitional variance happens with oral traditions over such a vast span of land and time. In this text *buddhi* refers to the more basic mentality, the intellect.

It is ego who adds the precondition, "Assuming that the physical world I see is outside of me, what is the most fundamental thing in it?"

Intellect would prefer to gloss over uncertainty and play in a world it can control, even if that means reducing the scope of life profoundly. Ego will do whatever is required to exert control and provide safety to itself.

This tendency to prefer self-limitation rather than confront the greater reality mirrors fascinating insights from **attachment theory** in modern psychology. It is now accepted that in cases where children have insecure or unsafe environments, their developing intellect prefers to establish the belief that "I am not good enough, it is my fault" rather than the more terrifying, "my parents are unreliable, the situation is out of my control, and they might hurt or abandon me."

Will We Liberate?

The way we respond to experiences of intense existential vulnerability is key. Even though all manner of ancient Eastern texts and modern professional cosmologists describe a metaphysical multiverse where all versions of all decisions are played out on parallel timelines and that objects can know about each other's states even when light years apart, people still behave as though solid things are real, intangible things are not real, and that words are the best form of communication.

Glimpses of the non-physical reality are euphoric for a while, especially if serotonin-boosting drugs are present during the epiphany. But afterwards, the ego tries to make sense of what it saw and regain control. It will always take the option it perceives as safe, and this usually means **not** solving the puzzle of its reliance on a mysterious light from beyond.

Similar to the case of the neglected child, our poor ego would rather accept limited control in a severely restricted world, rather than risking its existence to **see if** greater access is possible. It would rather be disappointed in advance than take the speculative leap.

So tricky it is to bring epiphany back to the world of words and objects, we tend to revert to old ways after the trip wears off. As a result, much of modern spirituality is just enhanced materialism. It presupposes separate physical forms, limited in time and space, but with a sprinkling of supernatural on top. It offers a mild boost for the material life, a poetic spin on hardship to help people persevere through the rough days.

Shankara, Aurobindo, and so many other Greats have come to Earth to shake people out of the material confusion. The work they did found fertile soil, and the text we are exploring here is a helpful boost.

The Seer, the everpresent witness, is the most fundamental thing. The intellect, the eyes, the objects, all exist on and by luminous conscious awareness. We have all the power we need to create a new Earth right now. This text explains how to do it using a regular practice of meditation, intention, and visualisation.

The Conscious Reversal

Śloka 8—11

अहंकारस्य तादात्म्यं चिच्छायादेहसाक्षिभिः
सहजं कर्मजं भ्रान्ति जन्यं च त्रिविधं त्रमात्

ahaṃkārasya tādātmyaṃ ciccāyā-deha-sākṣibhiḥ
sahajaṃ karmajaṃ bhrānti janyaṃ ca trividhaṃ tramāt

संबन्धिनोः सतोर्नास्ति निवृत्तिः सहजस्य तु
कर्मक्षयात् प्रबोधाच्च निवर्तेते त्रमादुभे

saṃbandhinoḥ sator nāsti nivṛttiḥ sahajasya tu
karmakṣayāt prabodhācc nivartete tramādubhe

अहंकारलये सुप्तौ भवेद्देहोऽप्यचेतनः
अहंकारविकासार्धः स्वप्नः सर्वस्तु जागरः

ahaṃkāra-laye suptau bhaved deho'py acetanaḥ
ahaṃkāra-vikāsārdhaḥ svapnaḥ sarvastu jāgaraḥ

अन्तः करणवृत्तिश्च चितिच्छायैक्यमागता
वासनाः कल्पयेत् स्वप्ने बोधेऽक्षैर्विषयान् बहिः

antaḥ karaṇavṛttiśca citiccachāyaikyamāgatā
vāsanāḥ kalpayet svapne bodhe'kṣair viṣayān bahiḥ

The infinite reality experiences itself by dividing in two, which implies a third. Just as the undivided idea contains subject, object, and verb, from the undivided state emerge subjectivity, objectivity, and activity. Interaction spawns time, space, and the physical universe. Material objects are presentations of the infinite, appearing finite, mixing with one another, all sustained by the absolute and infinite all-that-is.

Games and conversations become possible when finite subjectivity can discern finite objects. The human ego is a finite subject characterised by seeking and attaching to ideas and objects. While it **can sense** things larger and more complex than itself, ego **cannot control** such things. Faced with the choice of what to pursue, it often selects smaller and simpler objects. This action, while comfortable, stifles intelligence and rapidly cascades, reducing thirst for expansion, and potentially leading to the abandonment of the *avante garde.*

One may interrupt the slide and reverse the direction of attention. The shrinking tendency can be reformed using techniques of integration like *samādhi.* In practice, the habit is replaced by repeatedly noticing the reductionist assumption and making the decision to identify with the source of ego which is, by definition, outside the current scope. With practice, the vestige of belief in separation wears out and the scope of the ego increases. This is also called self-knowledge, *ātmabōdha.*

Aside from the *samādhi* practices described in this book, a convenient exploration is simply paying attention to what happens in and around sleep. Ego loosens partially as a person becomes unconscious, as they fall asleep, and things become more fluid. This is a direct demonstration of how identity can be adjusted relatively easily in a daily life.

Pay attention to how ego identifies with things when waking as well. When a feeling comes, the habit is to automatically claim it, as in "I feel great today" or "I am anxious today." But the decision does not have to be so consuming. Yes, the feeling is momentarily present – that is all. Sometimes things in our awareness are explainable, sometimes not.

We can and ultimately do always select our feelings. This can be more or less difficult depending on the person and the topic at hand, but it is a fundamental quality we all possess, and shortfalls in ability can be overcome. To do this, we start by defining and asserting a self-image that acknowledges our power of will and which elevates confidence in this native ability.

Discovery of the Subtle Body

Śloka 12

मनोऽहंकृत्युपादानं लिङ्गमेकं जडात्मकम्
अवस्थात्रयमन्वेति जायते म्रियते तथा

mano 'haṃkṛty upādānaṃ liṅgam ekaṃ jaḍātmakam
avasthā-trayam anveti jāyate mriyate tathā

We often assume that everything passing across our consciousness was created by our own brains. But we don't know that really, maybe they belong to someone else. Unexpected feelings can be agonising for the ego, they remind it of that strange other space, the wide open uncertainty. Right away it starts commenting and describing to fill the uncomfortable silence and establish a semblance of control. All that inner analysis is a distraction to avoid **feeling** what is present.

The techniques of *samādhi* help us properly **see** and **experience** the contents of consciousness as they arise in the **subtle body**, *antaḥkaraṇa.*[2]

The subtle body is **the real you,** and it creates your ego and body. Think of it as a large sphere of energy with your human in the middle. The heart of the physical body is the heart of the subtle body, and the whole field moves with you as you walk along the street, it goes with you left and right, *gauche et droite,* up and down.

Anything you can see with your eyes or touch with your hands is inside your subtle body. Think of it as having a 100 metre radius, with awareness strongly concentrated in the centre, and the edges tapering off gradually. Your subtle body overlaps the subtle bodies of other people and creatures nearby. Perception of others' energies grows stronger as you move closer to them.

It also contains more than just physical sense perceptions, mental constructions and emotional forms also reside there. Behaviours and ideas are sometimes introduced (or emphasised) from one person to another by sheer proximity, in silence.

[2] The subtle body has many names, including inner being and psychic self. In this text it is also referred to as *liṅgam*, a symbol of the manifest touching the unmanifest.

The subtle body spans time as well as space. Emotions you felt five minutes ago are still in the subtle body, and they usually fade away after a while. Things you are going to feel in five minutes are there too, coming closer to your present moment awareness.

Another defining feature is its **persistence** over the waking and dreaming states. Feelings move across worlds. Your subtle body is affected by your waking experiences, dreaming experiences, and the projections and behaviours of other people.

The subtle body is active across all of your days and nights. It lives longer than the physical body and it remains awake the whole time. It is more permanent and thus could be considered **more you** than your waking personality (the ego, intellect, *buddhi*).

Repetitive awareness and sustained identification with the subtle body is the key recommendation of this text. **The intellect's discovery of the subtle body is a huge milestone**. Now they can work together. The intellect can meditate upon the subtle body and a new self-image can evolve. The human being can expand out of the skull.

What a relief to have the contents of the subtle body recognised and made useful. It has always been a little jarring to push away those signals, such as feeling the tone of an event shortly before it occurs, or knowing something before being told about it. It is such a curious cultural phenomenon where people agree to ignore the eerie, often mutually experienced, coincidences of life.

This meditation sets the scene for life. It becomes the technique of every moment – noticing cues and signals as they occur, and sculpting moods and projections from an elevated position, with greater tolerance for things undesired, and greater influence than previously recognised.

Manifestation is Projection and Veiling

Śloka 13—15

शक्तिद्वयं हि मायाया विक्षेपावृत्तिरूपकम्
विक्षेपशक्तिर्लिङ्गादिब्रह्माण्डन्तं जगत् सृजेत्

śakti-dvayaṃ hi māyāyā vikṣep-āvṛtti-rūpakam
vikṣepa-śaktir-liṅgā-dibrahmāṇḍantaṃ jagat sṛjet

सृष्टिर्नाम ब्रह्मरूपे सच्चिदानन्दवस्तुनि
अब्धौ फेनादिवत् सर्व नामरूपप्रसारणा

sṛṣṭir nāma brahma rūpe sac-cid-ānanda-vastuni
abdhau phenādivat sarva nāma-rūpa-prasāraṇā

अन्तर्दृग्दृश्ययोर्भेदं बहिश्चब्रह्मसर्गयोः
आचृणोत्यपरा शक्तिः सा संसारस्य कारणम्

antar dṛg dṛśyayor bhedaṃ bahiś ca brahma-sargayoḥ
ācṛṇoty aparā śaktiḥ sā saṃsārasya kāraṇam

But there's more than pleasant psychology at play – this technique reveals the whole mechanism of physical manifestation. The ego is itself a manifestation, illumined by the Seer, beyond the material. The creation of bodies, intellects, and all other objects and entities takes place in a logical and describable fashion.

Manifestation occurs through a dual process of imaginative **projection** followed by **veiling** action (or labelling, deciding, voicing). The classic example from old texts is frothy foam in the ocean. We know it is the result of a process involving salt water, air, chemicals, minerals, and churning. This can be turned into something new and distinct by holding the image and form of it in mind, giving it a name, and then making statements about this now separate thing called "foam".[3]

Another example is the state of anxiety and doubt. In this state there are many negative **projections** present. They may be varied or there

[3] This wouldn't be a legitimate book on spiritual metaphysics without at least one mention of quantum physics, so here it is, be ready to cringe, scientists: Action collapses the wave function, taking the initial super-position of all possible paths, turning it into one path that is now considered "factual".

may be multiple repeated versions of the same troubling scenario. The trouble comes when you give up and **decide** you are no longer willing to sit with the uncertainty, no longer willing to try and bring yourself to the state of positive expectation. When you assume the negative outcome just to escape the torment of uncertainty, then ego can get to work planning for all the ways it could go wrong, adopting a state of vigilance, drawing conscious energy away from positive ideation.

You may even receive a dopamine reward of accomplishment for having made a decision, which reinforces the behaviour!

It would be better to let go and **let it be undecided** – even if difficult. Allow the image to rise and fall away again, rather than latching on and producing permanence. Life wants you to be open, let all scenarios exist as valid choices, and see that there are numerous positive possibilities to consider and nurture. You can choose to trust. This does not mean dropping attention or being careless, rather, it means yoking the intellect to the subtle body so they may signal to each other. Intellect needs to be observant, willing to act, and also **willing to release the reins**.

The first part of manifestation is projection in imagination. Forms in consciousness are amorphous and responsive to our multi-faceted perceptions and will. They become stronger with emotional investment and more elaborate with creative consideration over time.

The second part of manifestation is action in the physical. Behaving as though the projection is true or a voicing a firm decision, such actions make the previously adjustable form now seem permanent in time and space. Expression solidifies the idea and brings it under control of the physical. It is declared to now be "real", and the freedom to adjust the form is forgone. **It is said and done**.

Why would we relinquish that freedom? In the anxiety example above, it was to resolve the torment of uncertainty, assuming the unpreferred outcome just to ease the pressure. But we habitually and purposely relinquish freedom with positive things too.

Anything we dream can be created anytime in imagination, but long ago the human experience narrowed to a rapid succession of very small and similar moments. For good reason – things have a kind of magical fun when we forget we made them. So after each tiny projection, we "blink" and wake up again, over and over, with material reality just unfolding before our eyes. Such sharp and repetitive manifestation allows us to experience separation, alienation, and physical play. We cannot tickle ourselves, we can only be tickled by "other" people, and the degree of veiling creates a large enough gap to have sensory experience. We get to enjoy the relief of having finally made a decision that cannot be reversed, and the giddy thrill of touch and taste, and the pain of loss.

Working with Dreams

Śloka 16—17

साक्षिणः पुरतो भाति लिङ्गं देहेन संयुतम्
चितिच्छायासमावेशाज् जीवः स्याद् व्यावहारिकः

sākṣiṇaḥ purato bhāti liṅgaṃ dehena saṃyutam
citi-cchāyā-samāveśāj jīvaḥ syād vyāvahārikaḥ

अस्य जीवत्वमारोपात् साक्षिण्यप्यवभासते
आवृतौ तु विनष्टायां भेदे भातेऽपयाति तत्

asya jīvatvam āropāt sākṣiṇy apy avabhāsate
āvṛtau tu vinaṣṭāyāṃ bhede bhāte 'payāti tat

The subtle body who is awake in both dreaming and waking states is tantalisingly close to the highest supervising Seer.

A great place to be. The subtle body can participate in the empirical physical world, meaning it can observe and be observed. It can also stay close to the very highest witness and remain less attached to names and forms, soaring over them.

Aside from the full *samādhi* techniques described later in this text, dreams are a fantastic opportunity to peek behind the veil. We all know of the amnesia involved in the transition between waking and sleeping. If you can wake up a little during sleep and realise you are dreaming, you can open a gap and get a little more access. Likewise, if you learn to stay in the dream for a while after you wake in the morning.

Opening the gap between waking and dreaming does however remove a bit of mystery, as you realise it is make-believe. Whenever *māyā* reduces and more truth is seen, our sense of novelty drops a little. **Once you know, you know.** But dancing on these liminal edges can be a fascinating new adventure.

If you wake up from a dream and you want to go back there, it is simple to do so. Just close your eyes and remain very still. You can visualise opening a door back into the dream if this helps. When you first awaken, your conscious mind is still very close to the dream, and it is relatively easy to slip back in. If you have woken abruptly, you may find that when you fall asleep again you don't pick up at the same place you left off.

It is handy to know that the dream is always happening, whether you are conscious of it or not. Even when you are awake, the dream keeps flowing along. The subtle body is so large it watches your dreaming and waking states without effort. It is the ego that struggles with access, being easily distracted, but the connection can be developed by deliberately returning to the dream state right after waking.

Sometimes called *yoga nidrā*[4], this skill is strengthened with practice and it becomes important when accessing different kinds of *samādhi* states.

---

[4] "The transition between waking and sleeping can be expanded with *yoga nidrā*... A great deal happens in dream consciousness, but it occurs so quickly it tends to be missed. Such a large portion of life does not have to be lost in a haze. We can learn to maintain focus on the eyes-open and eyes-closed worlds at once... By dwelling at the borderline we develop a peculiar kind of concentration — as in a liquid concentrate, a pool of substance from which thoughts and actions arise. As one stops identifying with thoughts and actions, remaining focused on the subtle source, the concentrate increases... Non-physical sounds and visual content blend into barely describable nebulae within consciousness. Such ideations are the doorway to higher forms, so we meditate upon them. Spheres of consciousness are available to us that seem at times alien to the fixed physical personality with which we are accustomed." Pryor, Josh. The Spirit of the Matter. 2021

What of the Universe?

Śloka 18—19

तथा सर्गब्रह्मणोश्च भेदमावृत्य तिष्टति
या शक्तिस्तद्वशाद् ब्रह्म विकृतत्वेन भासते

tathā sarga-brahmaṇoś ca bhedam āvṛtya tiṣṭati
yā śaktis tad-vaśād brahma vikṛtatvena bhāsate

अत्राप्यावृतिनाशेन विभाति ब्रह्मसर्गयोः
भेदस्तयोर्विकारः स्यात् सर्गे न ब्रह्मणि क्वचित्

atrāpyāvṛtināśena vibhāti brahmasargayoḥ
bhedas tayor vikāraḥ syāt sarge na brahmaṇi kvacit

We have discussed the self-contained intellect which is prone to confusion about its dependence on external illumination. We have also explored the larger subtle body that perceives waking and dreaming states.

What of the universe? The universe, actually the multiverse, is called *brahman*. It is **all that is**. Everything that can be conceived of existing does exist and is within *brahman*. We think of "our" universe as having a specific history and future. This is a stance brought about by our friend *māyā*, the projection and veiling aspect, which compells us to focus on just one path rather than the infinitude of paths available.

We can dissolve the veils, and doing so results in greater awareness of options and coexisting timelines. It can be overwhelming, and when it happens too fast it is common to have a dark night of the soul[5] so profound that we again give up the uncertainty of infinite options and scramble to select any way out – even if only limiting paths are seen.

This text provides the solution. We can expand consistently and safely if we recognise ourselves as the subtle body **first**, before going all the way to *brahman*. Increasing the scope of awareness via concentration on the subtle body helps us acclimatise and work out the necessary changes to beliefs and self-image.

---

[5] The phrase "dark night of the soul" was coined by 16th-century Spanish mystic St. John of the Cross, in *Noche Oscura*. It is a well-known initial response to revelation.

We must know who **we really are** if we are to no longer to assume the identity of a brain-in-a-skull. Happily, in doing so, we transcend suffering. Our subtle body has information from other places. As we get to know the self who is always awake, we experience far greater quality of life compared to living via intellect alone.

It does not have to be esoteric. Make a list of positive scenarios relating to something that is consuming your attention. The default ego might say "this is dumb", but that is to keep you from stretching out to include the subtle body. It is protecting you from the unknown, the psychic self.

Everyone wins in these exercises. The intellect discovers the place where magic happens and realises that fear was not required. It can relax and be nourished into states that surpass materiality, where we have greater access to information and choice.

What of Other People?

We live in a paradox of autocracy and democracy – I am the eternal Seer, and so are you. We are each as infinite as our beliefs permit. When our worldviews are similar enough, they overlap like panes of glass and we share worlds. Reality is quite efficient in this way. But when perspectives differ significantly, separate versions of the world are created to enable the expression of individuality.

Some worlds are purely physical and dualistic, where survival is the focus, while others have different rules altogether. When the time is right, people seek out these alternate worlds and find other versions of loved ones there. To navigate this, just remember the primary rule:

> In every moment do the **most** exciting and interesting thing you can possibly do, as long as it doesn't infringe on another's freedom.

That word is bold for an important reason. Do the **most** exciting thing. Intellect will often take a relatively exciting path, but not the one most honestly desired. We must allow the compass of excitement to be known. It could be as simple as going for a walk, writing that idea down, doing a work task you had planned to do next week, calling someone who has been on your mind, or laying on the ground in a state of balanced contemplation. Assume the liberty of making decisions from the subtle perspective, rather than a superficially "rational" schedule.

By embodying this, we act as an eternal creator without the need to justify ourselves to the ego, and without a sense of entitlement toward other people. When you completely honour your own agency, you will always have everything you need to be in the state of enjoyment and flow, trusting that desires will be fulfilled in the best time and form. We offer opportunities to others when it feels right, and if they're declined, it's not an issue – we know they will be met elsewhere.

Back to the primary rule on the previous page. How can we possibly not infringe on another's freedom? We step on bugs all the time. Sometimes people enjoy having decisions made for them. Every dollar spent on personal comforts could be spent on improving the autonomy of disadvantaged people. It is a challenge to embody our own freewill, let alone understand where other people are at in any moment.

True, we cannot always avoid being the agent of someone's pain, but the trends are clear. People who grow old under materialism tend to become conservative and more willing to deprive others for their own sense of safety. Young people with less exposure to entrenched fear tend to reject war and genocide, and they value innovation over tradition. People who have suffered in life are sometimes desensitised to certain kinds of pain and unwittingly extend it to others. How best to take action without knowing how it affects the freedom of others?

Non duality provides the solution to this ethical conundrum. **All aspects of every action you take will be experienced by you**. Call it deep empathy. Sometimes effects will be obvious and immediate, other times delayed or abstract reactions that are difficult to trace. But everything you do is mirrored back to you in some way, and everything you are experiencing now has come from you. Thus, you are made aware of prior works in imagination, prior intentions and actions, and you possess **priceless feedback** that refines the ethical compass.

Shrinking out of fear is not the solution – **inaction is a form of action**. We see the negative consequences of complacency all around the world. It is time to stand up and re-assert our freedom, shape the world and enjoy every moment. Start moving! Learn by doing. This is a game you decided to play and no one emerges unscathed.

Ultimately, the greatest service you can offer others is the demonstration of faithful action from your highest passion, giving them a visible example of their freedom to choose.

२

Section Two

Śloka 20—32

Existence, Consciousness, and Bliss

Śloka 20—21

अस्ति भाति प्रियं रूपं नाम चेत्यंशपञ्चकम्
आद्यत्रयं ब्रह्मरूपं जगद्रूपं ततो द्वयम्

asti bhāti priyaṃ rūpaṃ nāma cety aṃśa-pañcakam
ādya-trayaṃ brahma-rūpaṃ jagad-rūpaṃ tato dvayam

खवाय्वग्निजलोर्वीषु देवतिर्यङ्नरादिष
अभिन्नाः सच्चिदानन्दाः भिद्यते रूपनामनी

kha-vāyv-agni-jalorvīṣu deva-tiryaṅ-narādiṣu
abhinnāḥ saccidānandāḥ bhidyate rūpanāmanī

All entities have five aspects. The first three are subtle and non-physical, combining in an ocean of sparkling potential, outlines of selves swimming like cosmic dolphins. They are **just barely** individual and they are abundantly aware that all the illumination and energy they experience is shared and free for all.

Those first three aspects are universal unconditional existence (*sat*), free-form projection in imagination (*cit*), and blissful enjoyment of the projected image (*ānanda*). **This is the subtle body**.

The other two aspects are name and form *(nāma-rūpa)* and they are what we perceive as manifested objects. **This is the physical world**.

Those first three are infinitely abundant and comprise the cosmic ocean of ideas. Shared equally by gods, animals, and people, the ocean holds the ingredients which can become events and objects.

A human can select ideas and have them manifest physically by **forming strong images and taking action with them in mind**.

This is the projection and veiling mentioned earlier. But the human condition is of such compulsive and unfocused speech-and-action that now almost no time is spent in creative imagination. Over a long time, society grew so preoccupied with tools, trade, and territory, that deliberate manifestation from consciousness became a dormant skill. Having become progressively more blind to *sat-cit-ānanda,* the focus shifted to consumption and production of things already existent.

The Open Heart

The connection between intellect and economics is plain to see. Insecurity and greed do not exist in the cosmic ocean, but they create war in the physical world and heartbreak in human relationships.

People with children experience how natural it is to love more than one person equally deeply at once, even to the extent that they would sacrifice their own life for the other. Humans have abundant capacity for all forms of love, and we are getting better at acknowledging this in society, but interpreting this in adult relationships requires an extra leap of faith.

Your child depends on you for survival and is unlikely to pack up and leave, but an adult could leave you **even if you love them**. So along comes fear and ego with contracts, compromises, and rules of moral virtue to give the perception of safety where it simply cannot exist.

Society is moving toward sharing, trust, and freedom. Beyond philosophical ideals, it is how our subtle body operates and interacts.

Previously, people had one job for life and one spouse for life, for better or for worse. This evolved and people became able to experience more than one job and relationship over the course of a life. Even more progress is now occurring where people are free to engage in more than one job or relationship **at the same time**, if and when they feel like it.

In personal relationships we move toward monogamy-in-the-moment, where we quell distraction and **be with** someone genuinely and sincerely in the present.

It can be challenging to grow into expansiveness and trust. The "Working From Home" revolution requires similar stretching. Employers learn to let go of micromanagement, and all parties are compelled to clearly determine and communicate their core needs rather than act from fear or suspicion.

A secure approach to life and relationships is committing to your own growth, knowing that **your radiance attracts all you need**. This confidence is self-perpetuating and offers greater safety and social benefit. This mindset is preferable to believing you must earn loyalty by impressing or serving a partner (although you may still enjoy that), or by trying to solidify the situation with marriage, children, and social reward.

Increasingly, social progress emerges from the influence of the cosmic ocean on the physical world, with the LGBTQ community playing a crucial role in our history. Despite facing significant stigma for their openness, they persisted and set an example.

Time and time again, new generations see the harm caused by fear-based social controls and appreciate the wisdom of more trusting alternatives. They naturally embrace this perspective while acquiring the skills and doing the inner work that comes along with such progress.

One person's gain is no longer another person's loss.

Exploring these practical matters is part of the spiritual journey. We are eager to switch to timelines that meet our ideal circumstances, but the human ego needs time to adapt. There may be unexpectedly strong beliefs to re-evaluate from a more universal and timeless perspective.

The Practice of Our Lives

Śloka 22—23

उपेक्ष्य नामरूपे द्वे सच्छिदानंदतत्परः
समाधि सर्वदा कुर्याद् हृदये वाऽथवा बहिः

upekṣya nāmarūpe dve sacchidānaṃda-tatparaḥ
samādhiṃ sarvadā kuryād hṛdaye vā 'thavā bahiḥ

सविकल्पो निर्विकल्पः समाधिर्द्विविधो हृदि
दृश्यशब्दानुवेधेन सविकल्पः पुनर्द्विधा

savikalpo nirvikalpaḥ samādhir-dvividho hṛdi
dṛśya-śabdānuvedhena savikalpaḥ punar-dvidhā

Having realised that all physical circumstances, *nāma-rūpa,* are the result of prior works in consciousness, a person should concentrate attention on the three aspects of imagination, *sat-cit-ānanda,* using *samādhi.* The main types of *samādhi* are *savikalpa* and *nirvikalpa.* They can be done any time, in meditation, in day and night dreams, and with open eyes.

In sleep we go there without much effort as ego detaches from the physical body, expanding to the subtle body. But in dreams we don't have much memory or control. *Samādhi* helps us go there while awake.

The dual process of projection in imagination and veiling by decision or action is happening right now. It is the means by which the universe is continuously manifesting. You are already doing it, but the tendency is to make a million small and very similar manifestations, rather than sculpting things new and significant.

These techniques help us become clear and honest **conscious creators**. Learning them requires consistent practice, and along the way they bestow all manner of practical benefit, including higher intelligence, peacefulness, and resilience.

Savikalpa samādhi is explained in the next two *śloka*. It can be conducted in two ways, to either learn about an object or situation, or to assert a desired feeling or situation. As we explore specific examples on the following pages, it is important to note that while the language used is modern, the techniques described are very old. Ancient texts are deliberately sparse and would quickly become obsolete if they contained examples from the time they were written.

The Current Feeling

Śloka 24

कामाद्याक्षित्तगा दृश्यास्तत्साक्षित्वेन चेतनम्
ध्यायेद्दृश्यानुविद्धोऽयं समाधिस्सविकल्पकः

kāmādyākṣittagā dṛśyāstatsākṣitvena cetanam
dhyāyed-dṛśyānuviddho'yaṃ samādhis-savikalpakaḥ

The first kind of *savikalpa samādhi* is where attention is directed to objects of interest until their full scope and source is reached, reducing the illusion of permanence, revealing their components and reason for being. Feelings of peace and bliss increase as initial concerns are replaced by a more complete perspective. All is seen and all is forgiven. Valid targets of concentration include things lofty as well as ordinary aspects of life such as moods, behaviours, problems. Here is a great trigger to start a meditation:

What gift am I experiencing right now and how is it guiding me?

Positive situations are perfect targets of concentration, but they can be easily missed. The ego considers them secondary to its real mission in life: self-protection. Nonetheless there are opportunities to allow expanded focus on things and people you love. For example, after the initial phase of attraction to another person, you may dwell in their energy, their scent and essence. Deepening beyond infatuation, physical characteristics seem to fade and we fall in love with their subtle body.

Negatively interpreted situations are useful targets of concentration too, although we often ignore them. Individual methods for dealing with negative experiences vary, and some are more visible than others. They include suppression and dissociation (easy to hide), as well as anxiety and panic (more visible). These are temporary remedies of course, they succeed only in taking the person one step away from the feeling.

In any case, with *savikalpa samādhi* we want attention rather than distraction. We draw things to us in life, and if situations or feelings keep arising, it means we have yet to extract all the information offered. Sour emotions and clouding of mind occurs when the ego holds a conflicting perspective to the subtle body. The pure energy is obscured by limiting beliefs. Discovering those beliefs is incredibly empowering, and the new choices offered improve life profoundly. Every time a painful emotion is felt, we know there is relief just behind the veil.

Feeling our feelings to their end is an act of high honour. It sets the scene for faster self-honesty in future, and the insights received help us discover and set our desired identity and state of being.

The *āsana* and *prāṇāyāma* routine within Ashtanga Yoga is a handy supplement, as it increases interoceptive awareness. This is the ability to detect subtle changes in the body and nervous system, helping us take prompt action to soothe the energy rather than flee the scene.

Definitions and semantics are so important when exploring belief systems. For years I was quite sure I had no negative self-talk. I never say mean things to myself, would never do such a thing! But eventually I realised the "tone of voice" in my mind was often negative, sarcastic, impatient. I was unwittingly denying the truth via technicality. It doesn't matter whether it's spoken in sentences, or if it's directed at others or at the self, it is still a toxin that permeates, creating confusion and anger.

Feeling our feelings to the end unites the ego with the subtle body, piece by piece, situation by situation. A worthy purification indeed.

There is an important nuance around the intellectual urge to explore personal history and "debug" ourselves. **We do want** to clean up the mind and **we will often** discover the cause of problems, but this is beside the point and can be a distraction.

To unite with the very large and non-verbal subtle body, we seek and attract the excellent feeling of knowing confidence. By pausing to consider good thoughts and preferred options, **we gradually expand and become the subtle body**. No talking, just incredibly useful information and bliss. Sincerely hold attention on the tumult until the spikes soften and our beliefs are exposed to light.

The Root of All Definitions

Every statement spoken or thought begins with "I am".

Whether implied or overt, every expression and action we make is accompanied by our personally chosen self-identity. So who is "I"? Some cultures consider "I" to be the brain and body. But it is quite reasonable to have an alternate definition, and this text recommends considering "I" to be the subtle body – the large sphere of energy with your human form in the centre of it. You can operate your life from this identity, you just need to remember to do so by frequent affirmation.

The subtle body is all ideas and all bliss. The little physical body dwelling inside will feel that energy permeating it, unless there is fixation on scarcity or similar limitations. Ignoring the greater reality creates tension, but with practice we can respond to that tension with "Aha! An opportunity to discover conditioning and reveal the pure energy behind it. What must I believe to be feeling this way?"

I am the subtle body, a sphere of positive energy radiating 100 metres in all directions, with a physical human in the centre.

With this kind of affirmation, we have the best of both worlds. The sensitivity and confidence of the energetic self is relished, along with the fleeting experience of humanity we love so much. The values, behaviours, and self-image of the physical person are more easily evolved from this comfortable and informed perspective.

An Example

If you have a sore toe, focus on it. Focus on the name and form, the sore feeling right now. Usually, we would give it attention for a little while it and then start hating on it or suppressing, getting angry or sad at it. But this time, feel the sensation for as long as it takes for the power of the pain to fade, rather than seeking distraction. Just sit there until it changes. Any experience gets boring after a while – including pain.

Do *savikalpa samādhi* by opening to the *sat-cit-ānanda* aspects of the experience instead of the name and form. Remember that manifestation happens via projection in imagination and a subsequent forgetting that you made the projection. Remove the veil by remembering that **you must have created this.** Own the situation and dive into the source. The degree to which you can see it squarely and receive all that it has to reveal, is the degree to which you can give it new ingredients and create a new preferred manifestation.

People discover all sort of things in this process. Any backing away, avoidance, impatience, limits this restorative and creative ability. It is all very personal and examples will not always be helpful. But for the toe it could be as simple as remembering the thing ten years ago that injured it, remembering the intensity of the situation. It might have been a single incident, or perhaps it was repeated mild trauma that you pushed through.

You could even trace the behaviour pattern to other areas of life. There may be something more significant that you can adjust. But beware being drawn away from *sat-cit-ānanda* by analysis, keep it brief. You don't need to intellectually solve the puzzle. That would be a bonus, but it can easily distract.

Once you have spent time in *sat-cit-ānanda,* rearrange the ingredients. Run that scene again with new intention. Behave differently this time. Pretend that this will change the outcome you experience in your toe. Act as though if you really believe it, the difference will be felt. Be patient and determined through the doubts and impatience of the intellect. It may be frightening to put yourself out there – to trust and be willing to take the risk.

The Desired Feeling

Śloka 25

असंगस्सच्चिदानंदस्स्वप्रभो द्वैतवर्जितः
अस्मीति शब्दविद्धोऽयं समाधिस्सविकल्पकः

asaṃgas-saccidānaṃdas-svaprabho dvaita-varjitaḥ
asmīti śabdaviddho'yaṃ samādhis-savikalpakaḥ

The other kind of *savikalpa samādhi* is where attention is directed to an energetically-infused affirmative statement so that it engulfs the mind. Here is a central affirmation:

I am a centre of consciousness that expresses the world, by creating clear images and acting with them in mind.

Qualities in the field of *sat-cit-ānanda* flavour our reality. Whether expressed physically or not, people have discernible habits of projection. Someone with a critical inner monologue presents differently to the world compared to a warm self-talker.

Moods have momentum and they influence others. The spheres of subtle bodies overlap one another with varying degrees of acceptance and resistance. Individual passions and vulnerabilities, firmness and flexibility, all intermingle to create myriad pleasurable, painful, and peaceful situations.

The mission of life is to understand and affirm who you are and then seek good feelings and exciting activities. **The things you desire need to be discovered and pursued**. That's why they are there! They excite because they are a part of who you intend to be in this life, and the energy around them makes it easier to bring them to fruition. Following your desire is the simplest and quickest way to self-actualise.

There is something we have always intended to do in this life. That thing can be known right now, but it is often buried. It is there, it does not need to be invented, but we often lose track of it in adolescence. By repeatedly turning away, we eventually forget.

Sometimes it feels so important to us—**too important to admit**—because if we found out that we aren't good enough or wealthy enough to pursue it, we would be devastated. Better to suppress it and go for easier things than face that heartbreak.

It's okay. Rediscovering purpose and power starts with this moment. Put aside the grand life plan and just honour the right now. What do you feel right now. What would be fun – a walk in the sun? And then the next moment the same question, over and over again. Re-learn the childhood skill of knowing exactly what you are excited by in each moment. Don't settle for less.

Statements of affirmation are an effective tool. Write the best idea you have for a present self-image and an intention for the near future. Affirmations are different to a diary entry, they have strong emotional content. They begin in imagination and culminate in a clear and charged statement of fact on paper. Write lots of them and be really bold and adventurous. Don't show anyone (unless you really want to). This is an integration tool for yourself and it must be a safe space for total honesty.

Keep writing who you are and what you are doing in this world as if there are no barriers. Thoughts of a certain theme attract more thoughts of that theme, write them and let them grow into clusters. If you feel bored by the task, you are being too general. If you feel overwhelmed or frustrated, that's a sign you are being too specific.

Limiting beliefs will arise as you write and consider statements. It is good to know what they are. Ponder their opposite, maybe they are untrue, maybe they were true when you were a child. Things decided in childhood become part of the adult worldview unless questioned.

Bouncing ideas off other people is important. Just as you cannot tickle yourself, there are insights that can only come from an inquisitor. Try expressing your beliefs out loud. Do it regularly, different parts of you are active on different days. You are evolving. The process could feel warm and gooey one day and inexplicably cold and intellectual the next. All versions are fantastic, keep doing it. We want continuous expansion of agency and self-knowledge.

Set up a **regular practice** of asking yourself what you want and how it would make you feel, and then writing it down and assuming it is true and already yours. This is **positive thinking**. We want to go beyond merely listing our cravings to writing affirmative statements of fact in the present tense as though they are true, even though the present circumstances seem *au contraire*. This is called **visionary behaviour**.

Check those sentences, check the words used. There must be no doubt implied, no waiting or wishing. No contingencies or clauses. Be clear and stubborn with the vision, but flexible with the details. What is the opposite of doubt? **We want that.** Wonderful attitudes can be reliably activated by changes to belief systems.

Momentum builds with frequent effort. After a while, the balance of action may shift somewhat, from writing statements to reading and feeling the confidence of those already written. This is a simple process of making positive emotions occur, but not many people do it... The uplifting ideas ought to grow more bold, occurring increasingly spontaneously. This is self-love, and it will make you strong and happy.

Visions should be re-touched many times a day. It starts every morning when you rise and make contact, transforming through the day, and culminating in the image held drifting into sleep. This is a lifelong practice of the wise. Write it on your hand. Listen to music with compatible lyrics. Sing and dance as that person with that feeling. Speak with the confident tone of voice of that specific person.

Are you willing to play the wild card, to act the fool? This is serious business. Historically, jesters were afforded special privilege to commit acts that would have others put to death. It would be a shame if fear of private embarrassment held us back.

Can you enjoy the intangible form, before the tangible comes? We can move sideways to the timeline of preference. Look for evidence that the world has changed, subtle messages of confirmation, demonstrations of fluidity. Start planning the **next things**, now the dream is here. Maybe even tell people about it as though it is true...

When you communicate with yourself like this, acting from a place of **unrelenting security**, then insights and ideas can reliably come from the strange other place. Intention setting and "shadow work" during retreats is great but, in the tradition of the *avadhūta*[6], the test comes when you don't expect it. That is when you will reap the benefit of having had a vigorous practice routine.

---

[6] "The word in Sanskrit for wild mystical rattling is *avadhūta*. It refers to a philosopher or ascetic who shakes free, kindles, or agitates. Yoga advocates using the body, breath, and manipulation of energy to disrupt stasis, sometimes taking students to the edge of physical comfort. It can feel like fainting — intoxicating and visceral — expressed with the word *mūrcchā*, meaning to swoon." Pryor, Josh. The Spirit of the Matter. 2021

Transcendental Point of View

Śloka 26

स्वानुभूतिरसावेशाद् दृश्यशब्दवुपेक्ष्यतु
निर्विकल्पस्समाधिस्स्यान्निवातस्थितदीपवत्

svānubhūti-rasāveśād dṛśya-śabdavupekṣya tu
nirvikalpas-samādhis-syāt nivāta-sthita-dīpavat

Lastly, *nirvikalpa samādhi* is where concentration and awareness expand to all corners and everywhere in between. Steady like an unflickering flame in a windless place, in pure darkness, with no reference points to measure the passage of time. You are every-where and every-when, you are the reality within which all perspectives exist – those preferred and unpreferred, those alien and familiar. Perturbed by nothing, this is the feeling of confident knowingness.

Our culture ranks happiness as "nice to have", but not essential. The prescription of this text is different. We require a state of non-resistant curiosity and positive anticipation in order to lift higher in consciousness. There is a certain kind of good feeling that comes when the ego opens to the subtle body. More than intellectual satisfaction and sense pleasure, it is spontaneous inspiration, energising flow, confidence and empowerment. We feel this way when we let go of judgement and **do what excites us**!

Rather than rely on physical situations to produce pleasure in the brain, remember that feeling truly excellent happens when intellect reaches honest agreement with the subtle body. The larger self has vast information and energy, and dreams manifest easily when we work together. The two techniques just described help us break the illusory permanence of things already-manifested by finding their subtle ingredients. With consistent practice, novel ideas appear, along with profound peace at the pace of unfolding.

Nirvikalpa samādhi takes us deep into the place where reality is crafted, and it is closely aligned with *bhāvanā,* the amplification of joy. This state can come spontaneously. The great Ramakrishna was known to fall into *samādhi* unexpectedly during the day, to the point where he had helpers walk beside, ready to catch him. Sitting is a good strategy too!

A little more practical – but you must make time for it. Procrastination or resistance to sitting in profound tranquillity is a clue that it would be incredibly transformative for you.[7] Sitting in silence with your eyes closed, no phone and no chatter. Just watching and listening.

Here is a good seed for meditation. Visualise the universe as a soup of ingredients, with your visions and paths being lovingly cooked for you. Expand your awareness to **see many versions** of your desired outcomes coming true, all the interesting and excellent ways things could be presented for you, so many it becomes difficult to choose one of them. **Expand again** to include other versions of you receiving these outcomes, male and female versions of you, past and future versions of you, beings you identify as family, here and on other planets. **Keep expanding.** You are the Seer in the middle and on top and below and on every edge of this multiverse. There are many people on many planets living happy and rich and meaningful lives, and you are the one watching.

I am the universal Seer who is reflexively generous to all.

Nirvikalpa samādhi enables the delivery of your personal affirmation, honesty, and desire to the cosmos. The ego separates from the physical in a manner implying profound trust that there is something beyond which is loving and safe. This is the ultimate act of faith – and efficiency. The expanse beyond will respond and assemble forms using the perfect blend of energies and elements, distant and near. You know the images will go where they need to go and touch the hearts they need to touch, without needing to see the specifics of how it all unfolds.

This particular *samādhi* is very important. After the two steps listed in *śloka* 24 and 25, understanding and then defining, we must complete the process and let it all go, send it out. To shift reality properly, we need

[7] Practically speaking, it helps to have a well-regulated nervous system and a body with a certain blend of flexibility and strength. Being able to sit cross-legged for a long time without twitching around is important, as is having a spine that can rest in a happy neutral position without fatigue. Also note that people sometimes feel fear from the swooning and fainting sensation that accompanies dissociation from the body. It can also trigger memories of abuse, neglect, or exposure to violence in childhood.

to completely withdraw from the current state and immerse ourselves in desirous rapture. This is the proper application of dissociation.

The intellect's fixation on the material world can be a real problem. The unreliable and ad-hoc manifestation experienced by classical humanity results from the idle consumption of entertainment and the unthinking admission of irrelevent, contradictory, or frustrated thoughts.

There are already existent things that we wish to continue enjoying! A great practice is to actively stoke **desire for things we already have**, paying close attention to the ease and comfort of already having it, so we may apply that same attitude to our dreams. To manifest new things, release from the vision with this confidence held.

Shift attention, *en masse*, to that which creates the future. The how and the when of manifestation are not relevant, and nothing will happen if we keep trying to intellectually connect the dots. Better to make the firm decision and then move on. Events and ideas come in sideways when we aren't thinking about it.

There are many formal and informal techniques to interrupt the intellect and re-orient, and some of them are deliberately shocking. The general principle of isolation and seclusion will reliably break us free from addiction to materiality and beliefs that bind. But the most accessible, and perhaps the gentlest method, is sleeping and dreaming – it is wise to hold affirmations in mind while drifting off.

Other methods include travelling or moving to a new town, riding a fast motorbike in a straight line so quickly that your eyeballs roll back, fasting or staying awake for several days, getting into fistfights on the street, performing standup comedy for the first time in your life in front of a crowd, or discovering alarming truths about your family history via DNA matching services.

The yogic breath-holding technique called *kumbhaka* will do it too, particularly the external version where there is no air in your lungs and you experience a feeling of imminent death that transforms into an eerie state of bliss. Similarly, *jouissance,* where pleasure is increased until it becomes painful, and then even further until it transcends both.

The Malāmatiyya are a 9th century Muslim mystic group who practiced transcending the ego (they call *nafs*) by not only directing their efforts to the higher self and living in ascetic poverty. They would keep that asceticism private and act unlawfully in public to attract scorn, thereby avoiding the admiration of villagers.

We need unsafe activities that take us close to the edge of material existence – to face some form of death or reboot. Otherwise, the intellect will keep clinging, slowing things down, talking nonsense in the head, obsessing over details, complaining about the past, and thereby distracting us from most of reality.

So much spiritual practice, including this approach to manifestation, ties back to fundamental lessons we teach our children: the cultivation of focus, impulse control, and delayed gratification.

The Universe Within Form

Śloka 27

हृदीव बाह्यदेशेऽपि यस्मिन्कस्मिश्च वस्तुनि
समाधिराद्यस्सन्मात्रान्नामरूपपृथक्कृतिः

hṛdīva bāhyadeśe'pi yasminkarsmiśca vastuni
samādhir-ādyassanmātrān-nāma-rūpa-pṛthak-kṛtiḥ

These techniques can be applied to any objects perceived as external or internal. *Samādhi* reveals the precursor beliefs, projections, decisions, and actions so that we can break the entrenched habit of living in ignorance, seeing **only the name and form**.

We must see the *sat-cit-ānanda* aspects clearly in our daily life so we can adjust them. The physical manifestation will likewise, automatically, change.

Any internal or external object can be a target of meditation. *Sūrya*, the sun, is a popular and healthy choice, as are the *cakra*-s. But any aspect of life is applicable, and it's smart to embrace current matters that stimulate or cause pain in life, since they already seize your attention.

This suite of *samādhi* techniques is very pragmatic and should be given great focus. Practice the steps described in *śloka* 24, 25, 26 in a cyclical fashion. Statement and beliefs will be revised as new perspectives and experiences come along.

By doing this, and by generally developing the habit of identification with the subtle body, **suffering is relieved while living a physical life**.

The Intermediate Space

Śloka 28—29

अखंडैकरसं वस्तु सच्चिदानन्दलक्षणम्
इत्यविच्छिन्नचिंतेयं समाधिर्मध्यमो भवेत्

akhaṃḍaikarasaṃ vastu saccidānanda-lakṣaṇam
ityavicchinna-cinteyaṃ samādhir-madhymo bhavet

स्तब्धीभावो रसास्वादात्तृतीयः पूर्ववन्मतः
एतैस्समाधिभिष्षड्भिर्नयेत्कालं निरंतरम्

stabdhī-bhāvo rasā-svādāt tṛtīyaḥ pūrvavan-mataḥ
etais-samādhibhiṣ-ṣaḍbhir-nayet-kālaṃ niraṃtaram

A person with their attention so fixed on *sat-cit-ānanda* that they are constantly unlimited is said to have attained the intermediate space. This profound absorption is marked by aloofness to the way things are, regarding that which is perceived by the senses as obsolete. This awareness is sought after and should be pursued without interruption, using any of the methods given.

I am free and the purpose of life is joy. The physical world is an effect of imagination, and I enjoy the panoply of options. When this is our experience, ego and subtle body are operating together as one.

Inertia is common when turning around to the innovative and cheerful images in consciousness, so we use already existing cravings to lure attention and build momentum in a new direction. Hope and fear are pure electric energy, just filtered by belief. They may be allowed to reveal who you intend to become in this life.

Notice conflicts between the things you want and your worldview. Conditioning can be surprisingly embedded. It often comes up in the form of sourness and non-specific bad feelings. Sit with it until the information comes. Beliefs can be as casual and seemingly common-sense as "everything takes time and hard work". A counter to this could be "the entire universe blinks in and out of existence every moment and the experience of continuity through time is no more than a tradition."

People often discover that on some level they don't feel they deserve what they want. This realisation is very important and will bring new desires and affirmations that are prerequisites for the initial one.

Many people feel ashamed of admitting what they want. It is important to recognise fear of the anticipated social response to our needs. It will spark a new prerequisite desire for society to be different in some way so that the initial wish can be accommodated.

Often our initially stated desires help us realise our actual desires. Fortunately, beliefs are just habits of thought that can be replaced by repeating new preferred thoughts. There may be a bit of time and discipline required to get things moving, but the results are as sure as your zeal.

Divine Will

Śloka 30

देहाभिमाने गलिते विज्ञाते परमात्मनि
यत्र यत्र मनो याति तत्र समाधयः

dehābhimāne galite vijñāte paramātmani
yatra yatra mano yāti tatra samādhayaḥ

With disappearance of attachment to the physical body comes realisation of the highest Seer. From there, whatever the mind imagines becomes manifest, and vice versa. At this point, it is crucial to behold *brahman*, and for this reason a teacher will usually be present.

The light of *brahman* is the eager and animating aspect of creation. Material forms are inconsequential compared to their source in consciousness. We need to see with the eternal light for it to be handled well by the ego. Without *brahman* it will be devastating. If you see a lot of mechanical workings without being exposed to the light, things can get rough. You need to be on a steady base, a deliberate creator, tuned to the solutions of your world and the joy of becoming.

The hybrid being, the combination of physical mind and the large spherical subtle body, is so much more glorious, helpful, and positive than ego alone. Imagine, then, what would be the lustre of the physical mind under the influence of *brahman*?

Every moment is here for positive creation, and everything looks good when you start with a clear definition of your fundamental identity.

The Lesson of the Fine

Hold attention at the source. Be a new person with a new future. It is not neccesary to know every detail of how things unfold, but we do need to know who we are now and then **act that way**. Actions are the details we can and should control, and this includes speech.

Inability to be silent suggests addiction to name and form rather than the cosmic ocean. A conscious creator behaves with care and deliberation. Does this need to be said? Does it need to be said now? Does it need to be said by me?

I tend toward exclusively positive inner conversations and ideas, which reflect in positive outer conversations and circumstances.

The energy of rehearsing arguments and complaining to yourself will accompany your daily actions. **We can hear you**. Even "innocent" habits like imperceptible frowning and scoffing may need to go. The insidious roots of the baobab trees will spread across the mind if permitted.

The best path is a positive focus on **feeling good,** rather than sternly monitoring thoughts. You deserve to be in harmonious alignment with the subtle body all the time, and the practice is to consider the thoughts and feelings present in each moment, and move them in the right direction. The fine details matter, where we know we are being lazy or irresponsible with the energy. There is no need to linger in self-judgement for feeling grumpy, just notice and consider the negative behaviour, and switch to something better. Become one of those people who wander around smiling charitably.

Latent annoyance with the seemingly external world must be resolved. Irritation at the public, people behaving badly, snarls in traffic, mass media, and social apps. These are reflections of the barbs of aggression harboured within yourself. This is all low-hanging fruit and it will either be transformed into elixir or it will rot on the ground.

It is simple enough to change the habit, perhaps difficult initially, and then it becomes great strength. We have the opportunity to act, internally and externally, from love and kindness rather than the historic prejudice of the ego. Leave behind old forms of restricted living, but as always, allow others to explore if they choose.

Psychosocial Safety

We want to be increasingly positive in physical life, and this means fine-tuning behaviours beyond present and obvious examples. We want to express the highest passion and most honest forms of excitement, while demonstrating sensitivity and respect. These things go well together.

In corporate settings, this is reflected in nuanced language that honours people across all cultures. The workplace is an important spiritual laboratory as it forms such a key part of life purpose for so many. It has been an admirable driver of cultural development.

As humanity bridges gaps and smooths rough edges across all the layers of society, we increasingly mirror the cosmic ocean, where there is no negative expression at all. But why clone the cosmic ocean in our human experience? What about the thrill of novelty, the unknown – the reasons we came here?

The whole point of being in materiality is to have experiences that aren't known in advance, and may be perceived as negative or positive. Contrast helps us determine what we want. Possibilities we signed up for upon coming here include: watching scary movies, bungee jumping, eating chocolate, trying out new recipes, running away from police, learning to handstand, and putting our legs behind our head.

In these activities we find risk and uncertainty, and it may not always go as we expect, but that's what makes it FUN — pushing beyond comfort and conservative control. We are here to be frightened and titillated, experiences not possible in the cosmic ocean.

Resistance to "wokeism" and political correctness in modern culture reflects this paradox. We want kindness and the absence of violence, but we also don't want to sanitise life. There must always be risk, without it life becomes dull and pointless. If material safety becomes the dominant factor in decision-making, there will be no exploration, and the process of evolution will short circuit.

The good news is that mirroring pure positivity in this world will not erase the natural properties of it. There will always be risk and novelty, but we can smooth the negative peaks, if desired. We can experience life like stepping into dramatic productions. Thrilling adventures that can be long or short.

The Fetters of the Heart

Śloka 31

भिद्यते हृदयग्रंथिः छिद्यन्ते सर्वसंशयाः
क्षीयंते चास्यकर्माणि तस्मिन्दृष्टे परावरे

bhidyate hṛdayagraṃthiḥ chidyante sarvasaṃśayāḥ
kṣīyaṃte cāsya karmāṇi tasmin dṛṣṭe parāvare

With awareness of the total self who is high and low and all around, tendencies of misidentified agency and externalised control are solved. The intellect abandons the habit of using matter to manipulate matter, and instead seeks union and co-creation with the subtle body.

The fetters of the heart are broken and confidence appears. You realise that all things already exist and you hasten the appearance of what you prefer by following the signals of excitement, going there in imagination, and acting in the physical world with the experience of having it already. It might seem normal to spend idle time monologuing in your head, but this is unhelpful. You must habitually honour and focus on what you desire, otherwise life slows to a crawl.

A doubt may arise. Is this just a trick to get us to stop fixating on the thing that's out of reach? Is all this attention on good vibes really a diversionary tactic to make us "just get over it", to focus on something new since the thing we really want doesn't seem to be coming? A classic belief of materialist culture is that "no-one gets everything they want, life is a mixed bag, sometimes you just have to move on." This sounds reasonable and it is a valid exploration.

But the prescription of this text this is different. You can be a consciously manifesting fusion of ego and subtle body, reaching into times and places that spur the outcomes you seek. For that to occur, the mind must be happy, optimistic, cheerful, confident, and trusting.

Why? Because you, as the large sphere of energy, extend far into time and space, and many more ingredients become intimate. There is too much content here for the intellect to reconcile, and if it attempts to analyse it is quickly overwhelmed, falling into distraction. Therefore, to remain expanded, all argument must be relinquished. Foster instead the unshakeable confidence that a positive attitude attracts solutions.

Grounding in Reality

Practice moving from negative to positive states. It requires strength and courage to stare down your unpreferred feelings and depressive habits. But we know that distraction and running away just delays the return. Better to experience temporary struggle than perpetuate the same situation for decades longer.

Movement to the positive state makes you strong and grounded in your true self, the large sphere of energy which houses the bones of the physical. It takes us beyond just coping with the delusion of materiality, reading nice books about spirituality, to actually inhabiting the preferred reality.

The resulting demeanour of self-trust gives everyone else a chance to contribute and co-author situations. Trust beyond your immediate physical context. This extra time is helpful. Make sure your ego is ready for what you want, not too frenzied. You would not want to fumble it at the last minute.

I am secure in the south pole, the north pole, and the molten core.

If you exist in this state, people will lift and match it as best they can. Sometimes you will find someone more positive than you! Match them – what a gift! Let's keep lifting the baseline mood for mutual benefit.

This brings us to the true meaning of *prāṇa* and our management of it, *prāṇāyāma*. Commonly associated with breath, *prāṇa* can be thought of as liquid light, and it fills the subtle body. *Prāṇa* is modified by positive and negative behaviour and is "exchanged" between people constantly. It usually is invisible to the five traditional senses but can be felt.

***Prāṇa* is simple enough to raise**. Methods include deep rhythmic nostril breathing, falling in love, moving through life in a state of appreciation, practicing yoga, singing in a choir etc.

There are many sneaky ways to drain *prāṇa*. Such behaviours include mouth breathing, excessive talking, miniscule expressions of negativity through gesture (sigh) and body language, gratuitous swearing and yelling, hyperactive twitching, insufficient meditation and rest, anger that is allowed to continue beyond its initial informative value, hurrying and rushing, aimless browser tab switching, wanton ejaculation in males, and uncontrolled or hysterical exuberance.

Aesthetics of Integration

Life is a song, a work of art. Aesthetics and skilful application of energy matters a great deal and therefore we practice visualisation more than talking. It gets easier the more you do it. Start by redirecting distraction, pick up your notepad instead of your phone. Bring the subtle body to the front.

The metaphysical necessity for joy is embedded in classical Ashtanga Yoga. There are ten behavioural guidelines to observe. The first two are the most important and they appear in a deliberate order.

The first one, *ahiṃsā*, translates as non-violence, but that really does not do the concept justice. We are already non-violent to a large extent. Yes, we still need to control our anger, stop hurting animals, and attend to hidden forms of limitation and doubt in our personality.

But it must go further again for us to expand and live in pure cosmic freedom. Caring about our state of mind is *ahiṃsā* and it is our ethical duty, individually and collectively. This is obviously the most important part of life and yoga. Any quality spiritual framework must prescribe the development of an eager and joyous mind.

The second one, *satya*, is truthfulness. This has a little more nuance in the context of these ideas. We have explored how there are infinite ideas we can select. Everything that can ever be dreamed up already exists, and is true for the people experiencing that reality.

Your specific path is illumined by the sense of excitement. It is harmful to suppress it or to take a path that would satisfy only the intellect, or only another person. Your power in the shared reality is to demonstrate freedom from material fixation so that others may see your example and know they can do the same. Whether deliberately selected or not, every action is consequential and ought to reflect the most sincere and authentic truth for you in the moment.

In this way, *satya* is a perfect partner for *ahiṃsā*. You are selecting a world that we may share, please do so consciously, and make it reflective of your true purpose. We want to enjoy your vision.

Make space for your honest desires to exist comfortably. When you spend significant time concentrating on things <u>other than</u> your physical conditions, you will live each day in a wonderfully exalted state. If you aren't walking around feeling that way, if you are a bit up and down, complaining, or a bit vague, it means there is more to be done.

The Highest Act of Courage

A person acting from their subtle body overlaps with many others in time and space. By consciously expanding well beyond the skin, that person becomes, in a sense, more than one person. They must operate smoothly with a far larger field, and being triggered by the presence of others would drop them straight back to limited physical existence. To maintain stable identity, they must be free of scarcity and competition. The syncretic personality will naturally insist that all persons have equal opportunity to explore the extraordinary beauty of life.

Appreciate the rest of your life. The areas that move so easily. The nice time we had five minutes ago, or five years ago, or any other time. So much has gone well! Being tapped on the shoulder by the memory of a bad time once had, or the fear of a bad time to come, can pull us back to the tiny piece of real estate that the ego can control.

Things are excellent. If the anxiety protocols aren't brought under control and re-shaped as aspiration and tenderness, we will keep falling from the sublime combined identity, and the whole project stalls.

The idea that everyone deserves pure abundance sounds like a new age platitude, and it can be, but there is a profound metaphysical truth:

Division from the infinite is the highest act of courage, and it is the reason that all wishes are subsequently fulfilled.

To any one who creates a unique self out of the absolute self, to any one who carves a circle in consciousness from which to emerge, to those who become separate so that the infinite may experience itself through the subject-object relationship, through duality and limitation – to those souls all subsequent choices are validated, deserved, and granted.

Leaving the unmanifest state so that *brahman* may have experiences is the boldest act, and this is what you have done. Thus, all freedom to choose desired paths and all right of return is bestowed.

Teachers and Great Ones

Śloka 32

अवच्छिन्नश्चिदाभासस्तृतीयः स्वप्नकल्पितः
विज्ञेयस्त्रिविधोजीवस्तत्राद्यः पारमार्थिकः

avacchinnaścidāmāstṛtīyaḥ svapnakalpitaḥ
vijñeyastrividho jīvastatrādyaḥ pāramārthikaḥ

Let us address some other selves. Here are three kinds of individual identities. One is the highest Seer, called *sākṣī* or *ātman*. Another kind exists only in consciousness, variously known as guides and oversouls. The third is the classical physical form.

Sometimes guides are called angels, nature spirits, and ghosts. Other times they are future selves and aliens. While unique flair and structure is observed among them, they all are centres of consciousness, as are we. Although similar to us, the concentration of energy in *sat-cit-ānanda* means they are usually invisible to our physical senses.

We all move in and around these roles fairly freely in dreams, where the fundamentals of identification, belief, and relationship are loose. Experiences are usually forgotten upon waking. In order to perceive other entities **while awake**, a human must arrange themselves to be a closer match. As with any manifestation, it starts in imagination.

Aliens and the others represent aspects in consciousness that we have tended to gloss over or repress. As science and popular culture start to confront that which has been pushed aside, things appear before us. The arrangement of collective imagination shifts, and all of a sudden symbols are noticed in the subtle body and the physical world.

There is a cadre of entities playing around us, looking on with amazement at our lives of veiling amnesia and gritty physical sensation. They have all the time in the world and one of their favourite hobbies is to interact with material beings. They always have our best interests at heart and are always willing to give clues in response to questions.

Feel free to include new forms in your own being, or notice they are already there. You can introduce centres of consciousness and have them become relevant. Communication flows more easily with practice and the use of symbolism. Writing with pen and paper is useful as a means to spotlight ideas amid the mix of thoughts bouncing around daily life. Associating messages with deities[8] works too.

The key is clear intention. Give yourself permission to experiment. Cobble it together, that's all anyone does! We are a mishmash of cultures and genes, some that we know about and some from very different places. Consider our post-human descendants, hundreds of years from now. When this planet is full of and surrounded by people who developed the ability to stretch and relocate themselves in time and space, will you make yourself known to yourself?

Heroines are needed here. The masculine urge to escape the matrix and transcend this mortal coil is quickly cut short when truth descends. The drama of light versus dark and tales from mythology describe the experience of people who had proudly proclaimed they were ready.

Imagine hundreds of subtle bodies who are married together, having formed very long term relationships. Just like any one subtle body, they are peaceful and loving. Joined together they are purely positive, but their energy and knowledge is exponentially greater. They can serve thousands of physical egos. A cluster of subtle bodies becomes something else, something even more fine, reaching still closer to brahman. We can call it an oversoul.

Hearing the calls of prophets and mystics, on occasion they respond with presence. The human who beckoned them is rapidly lifted, their subtle body now infused, translating the paths and truths of so many more entities and realities. If the person has not deeply pursued their own limiting beliefs with techniques like *samādhi*, the wave of awareness triggers great fear. With compassion, the oversoul pulls away, leaving the human with partial visions.

In our culture, the classical female personality is often better suited to withstanding the impost of such experience, having been conditioned to hold on and be quiet when things get intense. For this reason, even though history records the testimony of mostly male seers and religious figures, there are many more who were and are women.

Ultimately, it is a part of you, coming through you. Regardless of names, the channel opens and everything folds into one identity.

---

[8] "Indian *deva* are collections of ideas for humans wishing to evolve. They are containers for non-verbal intentions, geometries, relationships, metaphors. They exist to rouse ideals, moods, concepts of being." Pryor. The Spirit of the Matter.

Love Incites Knowledge

There are connections and channels between all levels of consciousness and matter. When humans are immersed in nature, conscious communication is sent along paths that existed long before language. It is sincere loving interest that opens the door to all forms of contact. You can stretch into the centre of a large mountain, or sit inside a tree or a leaf. You can link with a raging storm and experience the rejuvenation of such extravagant cleansing.

Key to this is the concept of **identification** – conjuring the feeling of an entity or a place and making the confident and happy intention to connect. There is no real technique other than that. Love and excitement, confidence and desire, are the forces behind all movement of energy.

We can add connection to nature as a tool for expansion to our kit along with affirmation, playful action, meditation, and all the new habits we are cultivating. Modern culture is so sharply focused on material forms and busy schedules, our lives will be completely possessed if we do not create multiple avenues for aspirational feeling and intention.

Contact is invited with curious and loving intent. A sense of theatre and imaginative play is required – this is the language of *sat-cit-ānanda*. Of the whole unified existence, only 1% is *nāma-rūpa* and the other 99% is imagination. When you "go to sleep" and let go of name and form, you actually wake up into the bulk of reality. In the morning when you "wake up", you begin dreaming the limited physical experience.

Spend time every day sitting with your eyes closed. Fantasise and make projections in mind while considering the affirmations you have written down. Such rebelious non-physical action, when done for more than a couple of seconds, changes the shape of reality.

Texts of non-duality are often translated as saying that "this world is nothing but a dream". More accurately, they say we should consider this world to be a **lucid dream that we act within**. Isn't that what we would all love, to be able to control our dreams? So do it!

Rather than acting as a victim of the external world, act as if it is born from imagination. You are free to imagine anything you like, and hold it in mind as you go about your daily life, watching tones and themes change, just as in dreams. This experience becomes so enriching that the waking dream and the sleeping dream meld together into one state, and **life is experienced as the transition itself**.

३

Section Three

Śloka 33—46

Stars in My Eyes, Stars at My Feet

Śloka 33

अवच्छेदः कल्पितस्स्यादवच्छेद्यं तु वास्तवम्
तस्मिन्जीवत्वमारोपात् ब्रह्मत्वं तु स्वमावतः

avacchedaḥ kalpitas-syādavacchedyaṃ tu vāstavam
tasmin jīvatvamāropāt brahmatvaṃ tu svamāvataḥ

The individual is an imaginary circle drawn within infinite reality, and we call this the subtle body. It remains full of and immersed in consciousness. The shape sustains the sense of individuality and a point of focus while illumination permeates inside and outside. In each moment, humanity reconfirms physical reality, by selection, based on what it sees in the circle. The appearance of linear and continuous passage through time and space is maintained by the habitual selection of small moments that are very similar to each other. This narrowing of moments is an enduring yet optional tendency.

I am the Seer, aware of many options,
and every time I blink I set that which is real.

We can access any knowledge and any person if we are flexible and possess the conviction. **Knowing this, who would you like to be?** Doesn't have to be a person with a name. What do you want to embody? Write a few phrases, traits, and talents that excite and challenge you, things that would be almost too good to be true. Be daring. If you are not confident that what is described above will work, just apply the practice in a regimented and sincere fashion to prove it.

What would be the consequence of proving this to yourself? Most of us grew up under an unquestioned and fallacious worldview, and to rattle it after decades of comfort might be too much to bear.

Cultivation of a self-image that **knows it has and inherently deserves universal agency** is crucial. There is a common fable of a person who was broke, won the lottery, and ended up broke again after a year, unable to step into a new and prosperous identity.

Consider that even after years of hard work, carving a respectable life after childhood adversity, the seeds of pain, *saṃskāra,* from long ago may remain. You may not have exposed them enough, or at all. You pushed through, and the world validates your success at every turn, but what beliefs lurk deep inside? What *karma* remains unresolved? So many people live with the hidden **suspicion** that they are fundamentally broken. The fear of one day really **knowing** it to be true compels them to achieve in the world. Constantly pushing themselves to keep the fear at bay.

A self-created self-image based on metaphysical truth is the greatest asset. These are the issues we want to explore. If you are not in mortal peril right now, if life is kind of stable, then drop everything and become the subtle body, become the Seer.

Do you know why you are the obvious perfect choice for your lover, your job, and your dream life? If you would like others to value all the rare and irreplaceable qualities you possess, it is helpful for you to know about them first. This is nothing more and nothing less than self-love and self-knowledge. It is true that people often discover their virtues by accident or by external validation, that works as well, but it is unconscious and haphazard. The facts of who you are should roll off your tongue with warm conviction.

If you really aren't comfortable directing all this attention to yourself, you could start with service to others! Spend time reducing chatter and increasing visualisation of excellent circumstances for your friends. You could do it with strangers in the street too.

Picture yourself bathing in unlimited universal love, having it flow in and around you, and then see it as a golden flow from your heart's centre to the heart of another. Some of your own being will enter and warm the heart of the one to whom you send that energy, and you will experience the joy of offering and being a channel for universal love.

When you enthusiastically and unconditionally accept everyone and the path they see fit to take, you mimic God.

Remain Faithful

Śloka 34

अवच्छिन्नस्य जीवस्य पूर्णेन ब्रह्मणैकताम्
तत्त्वमस्यादिवाक्यानि जगुर्नेतरजीवयो:

avacchinnasya jīvasya pūrṇena brahmaṇaikatām
tattvamasyādivākyāni jagurnetarajīvayo:

A PERFECT DUPLICATE OF God is God. Consideration of the Seer in various forms and as various people creates disarming paradox for the intellect and is thus a valuable tool for liberation. Beware excessive rumination, we would rather not be stuck here for eons in ignorance of the illuminating source. This riddle will not be solved by intellect alone, it ponders the question and makes the request, but the solution is delivered by the hybrid being.

I am the immortal being through which states pass. Vedic *śāstra* and all manner of primeval and spotless teachings affirm this. The imperative is to discover this knowledge and verify it for yourself. Take responsibility for selecting the feeling you want. Be brave. In moments of pressure or distraction with a busy life it is possible to crumble and forget it all. Similarly, when you are comfortable in life and no calamity urges you to improve – back to your old ways. While ever this risk exists,[9] regular maintenance of the decision is the priority.

I am always willing to drop everything and do what is required.

Concerted and earnest effort makes us bounce in moments of fatigue. The cliché of university study is that the information is often unused, while the real value is learning **how to** stretch our minds with regular effort in a direction that is not always fun. Learning to concentrate and expand is an exercise that pays off. So, be proactive and write some new affirmations. Is there anything you can do right now to enhance the comfort and joy of those nearby?

[9] Spoiler alert: the risk always exists

You are Only Psychic for the Positive

Śloka 35

ब्रह्मण्यवस्थिता माया विक्षेपावृतिरूपिणी
आवृत्याखण्डतां तस्मिन् जगज्जीवौ प्रकल्पयेत्

brahmaṇyavasthitā māyā vikṣepāvṛtirūpiṇī
āvṛtyākhaṇḍatāṃ tasmin jagajjīvau prakalpayet

THE POWER OF *māyā*, projection and concealment, comes from *brahman*. With this power, universes, perspectives, and bodies are created.

Remember your freedom and re-manifest your world. Be willing to see and re-process trauma arising and choose a new path. Replay your life with this wisdom. You can choose a different past and live that life, becoming more of who want to be this time around. You may tell yourself that you have a certain past and that it makes you do specific things, but you could just as easily define yourself anew.

All memories are made in the present and **right now is the only time**.

It might be easier said than done. Our imagination is usually nimble in childhood simply because it hasn't been neglected at that age. Also note that being told you can fix everything if you just imagine hard enough can be irritating or even toxic. This is why we start gradually, pick something that seems reasonable and work with that. A playful approach is best, it brings speedy rekindling of creativity and provides a buffer for frustration.

Once the desire is clearly identified along with the feeling of it being here, we take it off the pedestal and get to work on other things. Does acting as though it is true feel delusional? Good! Think of it as theatre. This is how reality works and we are already doing it. We decide the permanence of perspectives. **The actor must believe the role he plays.**

There really is no other way. A mixture of confidence and victimhood does not bode well, we are already experiencing that as a blend of dilute impulses manifesting haphazardly. From here we can decide to use our power to create consciously 100% of the time. Otherwise, we are using our unlimited power to pretend we have limited power.

Psychic functioning is quite normal and already happening. As the practice of attending to the subtle body progresses, sensitivity and quiet space expands. Experiences of anticipating the future or knowing that something has happened increase. Like seeing or hearing a flash that is true or comes true.

Being psychic is possible and you can be that, but you must aim far higher. If simple personal advantage will satisfy and cause your practice to ease, the intellect will go crazy after a little while. Upon seeing such a radical tool, it gets thirsty. Superstition and paranoia will knock on your door. If you hunt for psychic skills from the perspective of a small being inside a large and threatening world, it is **game over for you in this life**.

The reality is that you project and create everything. Gaining advantage over another is foolish, like trying to steal from yourself. All things are from you even if you don't remember. It becomes increasingly important to make time for **aspirational creative meditation**. Even if the spiritual journey started in response to difficulties in life, we need to go beyond healing to proper upliftment.

It may be helpful to learn that negativity really only occurs in material existence – such gestures and words are easy to spot. There is an abstract form of negativity in the subtle body too – sour moods can be felt by others, but they taper off with distance. Higher again in the cosmic ocean, higher than the subtle body, negativity goes to almost zero. Identity alone remains, and it has just one negative aspect by definition, "I am this and thus **am not** that".

The point of view of an entity with barely any negativity is so different to our familiar human frames of reference, it can come across as sociopathic. The difference between crying from loss and crying from joy is not always clear from the cosmic perspective. You're feeling intense attachment to your love, isn't that what you want?

Journalling and affirming helps to define your parameters. Always be positive. Focus on what you **do** want. If you stop physically expressing negativity with words and actions you already cut out most of the trouble. Unloving thoughts and moods still need to be brought in and transformed, but that's much easier when you have stopped acting them out and mechanically perpetuating them.

Intrusive Thoughts

Recurring doubts and unpleasant interjections in the mind highlight new intricacies for contemplation. They can present new questions or inner contradictions to your vision, angles you hadn't properly considered before. Digging into beliefs can take some time and reflection. We can always sit with the feelings, perform *samādhi* on them, calm the body, focus the mind, and allow the truth to come forth.

Sometimes intrusive thoughts represent something more basic. They can highlight that the momentum behind the habit of trying to anticipate danger in advance, by vigilantly thinking about possible negative scenarios, is still active. If you have been doing this for many years, then a sustained effort is required to set the new direction. Gladly, every disruptive thought can serve as an instant trigger to switch to the positive. You have the tools, grab your notepad and turn this spare energy upwards toward the intention.

Worry is a very real addiction and should be treated seriously until resolved. If doubts or negative scenarios come to your mind, you can in fact reject them immediately and forcefully! That is needed at times. Recovery from addiction can be tough, but deliberately refusing an old behaviour that induces an inferior pleasure makes you stronger every day. We are retraining the wounded parts of our precious human self. The child who learned that being a pest gets results, or that negative attention is better than nothing at all, or that being paranoid is easier than sitting with the feeling that our innocent life is actually insecure and unsafe.

When negative compulsions have been around for a long time, they can almost be treated as another person, since personality is just a cluster of belief and behaviours. In those cases, they can be spoken to and befriended, and are often satisfied by love and acceptance, enthusiastic inclusion in the team of the whole person, and new games to play.

Return to the vision you have defined and the feeling you have selected. Imagining creative versions of your visions is a fun activity in itself. Much better than looking for trouble. There are so many ways your dreams can come true! If you imagine one hundred positive scenarios, it's likely that none of them will be the eventual outcome. But the persistent effort will have brought the energy of all positive paths to you, **and made you very happy**, and thus an effective creator.

The Voice of the Silence

Śloka 36 - 37

जीवो धीस्थचिदाभासो भवेद्भोक्ता हि कर्मकृत्
भोग्यरूपमिदं सर्वं जगत्स्याद्भूतभौतिकम्

jīvo dhīsthacidābhāso bhavedbhoktā hi karmakṛt
bhogyarūpamidaṃ sarvam jagat syādbhūtabhautikam

अनादिकालमारभ्य मोक्षात्पूर्वमिदं द्वयम्
व्यवहारे स्थितं तस्मादुभयं व्यावहारिकम्

anādikālamārabhya mokṣāt pūrvamidaṃ dvayam
vyvahāre sthitaṃ tasmādubhayaṃ vyāvahārikam

Material incarnations persist by repetitive affirmative action. But lives of expanded awareness and grace can also be imagined, so they must also be available. It is only for assumptions, "I am my intellect" and "the world is outside of me", that the monotony continues.

Repetition is key to building momentum in a new direction. We do all this visualisation to facilitate the easy and voluminous repetition of our intention and desire. We become a vibrational match to the presence rather than its absence. Thus, we live the *mantra*.

The experience of duality is a fun time and can be even more so when we correct the mistaken identification and recognise the full scope of reality. Adjustments can be made in ways thought impossible. Complete existence is where intellect is aware of its partnership with the subtle body and its condition of perpetually bathing in the light of *brahman*. By comparison, bouncing around in material chatter is like rubbing sticks together to start a fire.

There is a relentless stream of positive evolutionary sound and light raining upon us at all times. It is always available. But the isolated intellect perceives the light as an external threat and barricades itself. It creates doubt and distraction, errant thoughts that keep us unsure and off balance, hesitant to cast a long gaze. Habits that make us "safe" in a small prison, reflexively turning away from so many exciting options. Life is too complex for ego to manage alone, and thankfully there is a greater creative intelligence to partner with.

You Don't Have to Worry

Be not burdened with the **task** of positive imagination, either. Obsession can intrude on the innocent joy of exploration. Once desires are identified and compatible beliefs are set, the focus should change to resting in happy, positive expectation. Knowing that "slowly, slowly, all is coming" and with the conviction that you deserve to feel good, the process of manifestation can occur in fewer discrete moments of time.

It is counter-productive to hold on tight once the decision is made. Checking to see if it is visible yet or fretting about when it will come adds tension into the projection. You have worked hard, and now it is just as important to let go and allow things to fruit, away from your personal sensory experience. You might get to see some things formulate right before your eyes, but much of it will happen while you're out living your life. Enter a calm and clear state, go into the silence regularly. What do you want to do now?

Use Ashtanga Yoga to increase brightness of spirit and ease of relaxation. Consistent practice of *āsana* and *prāṇāyāma* most days of the week for many years develops well-regulated energy, and allows you to lift to ethereal calmness or sink into volcanic heaviness at will. Make it part of your life, like brushing your teeth. The bones and fluids of the body enjoy rhythmic movement and regular flossing. Physical yoga is the very best thing we can do in the current paradigm to blend and smooth our passion and energy to take us where we want to be.

Become quiet and **listen to the voice of the silence**. In yoga this is called *nādānusaṁdhāna.*[10] Learn to notice what emerges. She is subtle and she is here in every moment, becoming **very loud** the more we listen. She is attraction-based, and self-pity will not be well received. We have a relationship to build. Even when the relationship is brilliant and shiny, the messages can come at unusual times or in strange forms.

The end state of this meditation is undivided attention, blissful appreciation, and unmitigated eagerness for more – without fear of loss or *planning* for more. Pure grace in the presence of the Goddess is confident and generous without entitlement or grasping.

---

[10] *"Oh Goddess nāda, how glorious! We petition you to deliver access to the subtle causes while living this material life."* Yoga Tārāvalī *śloka 4*, The Spirit of the Matter.

Simply appreciate[11] that she is here, that we have the pleasure of her company. Savour her, it may be the last time. The universe blinks in and out of existence a million times each second. **It is always the last time.**

Like all relationships, it is a two-way street. We want the voice of silence to speak to us and we must also speak to her. This is done by making time for presence in imagination and effort to feel the highest feelings, even if it is a struggle at first and even if they are scary at times.

The Goddess lives on the edge of uncertain excitement.

Seclusion and the City

This was easier long ago when the world population was small, people were dispersed, and everyone understood the subtle layer. In that environment, the physical body (which talks to people and touches objects) and the expansive subtle body (superimposed over people, trees, animals, and others) coexist peacefully and harmoniously. This natural situation allows heightened sensitivity without much discomfort or unpleasantness.

When this peacefulness exists and a person approaches, even if they are not yet visible, one would typically get a sense of their energy. The emotional state shifts because the subtle body now includes a new person with their own mood. It was an idyllic situation. People moving around, their subtle bodies more or less overlapping, and the choice to move closer or farther away based on vibe, well before the physical bodies are directly involved.

As the global population grew and villages began to form and expand, the *yogi-s* of that time noticed that people's innate awareness of the subtle body was diminishing. Individuals had less time for themselves in tranquil and open natural surroundings. People were being born in densely populated areas, immediately entering the world with their subtle body intertwined with those of numerous others.

Ayurveda and the Upanishads emerged as a protective response to this crowding of bodies and scattering of attention.

---

[11] It is tempting to use the word gratitude, but it has been sullied by association with scarcity and having favours granted.

Today, it's possible for someone to go for many years affected by the energy of others, **never once** experiencing pure solitude.

Unwittingly sharing your subtle body with countless strangers for decades is perhaps an unsettling idea, and it gives rise to musings on boundaries and consent from an unusual perspective. No longer can you close the door to your apartment and assume complete isolation. Emotions are no longer entirely private; they impact and are impacted by those around you.

Suddenly, ethics takes on a whole new dimension. Cultivating inner anger or despair becomes rather inconsiderate since it affects your neighbours, even if you do not physically express it.

Remediation occurs by moving your body away from other people. It's good to choose a forested location with natural elements that have evolved alongside human biology. Just be there, alone, without distractions or machines. Activities like planting trees or caring for the land are a great way to sink into the experience. Make sure your mobile phone is turned off or far out of reach during this time. Even better to have no coverage at all…

If you've been sharing your space with countless others for years, you might need to do this practice more than once. The more the better. An overnight stay every week is very effective. Does that suggestion provoke a limiting belief? If you're seeking fast results, it's a good target. Note also that it's likely you'll carry the thoughts of others with you, but those thoughts will fade after a while when they run their course.

Your true self is already calm. Calmness is not something to acquire, but something to recognise in your centre. As capacity for self-regulation and your positive self-image unfolds, methods for preserving the delights of seclusion while living in the city become apparent.

The subtle fields of your neighbours overlap with yours, whether you like it or not. Even if they're not your usual type of company, you are engaging with them by proximity alone. Becoming wilfully familiar with others allows you to recognise their thoughts. Find the best and most positive aspects of their personalities and speak to that. Speak to the aspects you would like to see grow. A smiling "hello" goes such a long way – rural people who never lock their doors know all about this.

The Sādhana of Criminality

Śloka 38 - 39

चिदाभासस्थिता निद्रा विक्षेपावृतिरूपिणी
आवृत्य जीवजगती पूर्वे नूत्ने तु कल्पयेत्

cidābhāsasthitā nidrā vikṣepāvṛtirūpiṇī
āvṛtya jīvajagatī pūrve nūtne tu kalpayet

प्रतीतिकाल एवैते स्थितत्वात्प्रातिभासिके
न हि स्वप्नप्रबुद्धस्य पुनस्स्वप्ने स्थितिस्तयोः

pratītikāla evaite sthitatvāt prātibhāsike
na hi svapnaprabuddhasya punassvapne sthitistayoḥ

In sleep we have a demonstration of our ability to create, with imagined forms rising and falling. In meditation this skill can be developed. Recede into the heart as though falling asleep, and wake up into the reality of *sat-cit-ānanda*. This world is for experimentation and it was created by you in the spirit of frolic. Dreams can be intense and scary, but they are easily forgotten and replaced. So too with this.

Sometimes spirituality looks like peaceful healing, and other times **it is outright criminality**. Yoga was illegal in Romania in the 1980s. Homosexuality was illegal in most countries and remains so in some. Abortion was illegal around the world and occasionally becomes recriminalised. Cannabis was illegal in many countries but is becoming legalised and normalised. Psychedelic mushrooms were illegal and are now being introduced as therapeutic tools with great success. It used to be legal for a husband to do as he pleases with his wife without her consent. The slave trade was a completely normal part of life all around the world. Torture is still practiced by developed nations.

Of course there are many more examples of unjust laws. The prevailing worldview claims ethical authority and it succeeds as long as people agree to hand it over. Cultural evolution occurs when people who are sufficiently motivated to go against the grain of society do so with courage. Everyone shares the benefits equally.

Laws, commandments, social norms, parental guilt-trips, traumas from childhood are all ideas. Some conventions align with common sense and our personal convictions, some do not. How much conformity to accept? **We are evolving**. You are subject to no law, there are no rules in your imagination. We each have the power to dream up new ideas, new laws, and then act with them in mind. Take an active stand against limitation. Outrageous, the way it perpetuates for generations.

I salute the social outlaws.

Romancing the Goddess

Śloka 40 - 41

प्रातिमासिकजीवो यस्तज्जगत्प्रातिभासिकम्
वास्यवं मन्यतेऽन्यस्तु मिथ्येति व्यावहारिकः

prātimāsikajīvo yastajjagatprātibhāsikam
vāsyavaṃ manyate 'nyastu mithyeti vyāvahārikaḥ

व्यावहारिकजीवो यस्तज्जगद्व्यावहारिकम्
सत्यं प्रय्तेति मिथ्येति मन्यते पारमार्थिकः

vyāvahārikajīvo yas-tajjagadvyāvahārikam
satyaṃ prayteti mithyeti manyate pāramārthikaḥ

What seems most serious is often the least important. The things that carry innocence matter most to the inner being, the little prince, and they are frequently invisible. The child of vision explores the world of planets and people, physical forms he considers ephemeral, playful, and easily changed. All the while longing to again hold the invisible energy behind the stars, the source of their beauty.

Innocence is an ideal complement to the awkwardness of a life that no longer strives for efficiency and safety. Innocence allows the ego to peer through built-up doubts and participate in the ecstatic state of all that is. Things seen with the eyes are the past, the state of our heart is the future.

Romancing the Goddess is the practice of holding the mood to match the subtle body, and observing what comes through without being unsettled.

You must be okay being vulnerable over and over again. Not knowing the specifics. The longer you live in the zone of tormented uncertainty, the more you discover it is actually the zone of ecstasy. The intellect does not initially understand how serving at the feet of the Goddess could be anything other than torture. But it learns to sacrifice control and in doing so finds itself bright, happy, and in love. **This is *yajña*.**[12]

There is a time for the ego to take the lead and provide experiences. But in highly motivated materialist culture, "completing tasks" can easily dominate the behavioural landscape. Sleep is the evolutionary circuit breaker, ensuring the ego is disarmed at least once a day. In order to fulfil our dreams and successfully unite ourselves, we must make the effort to more frequently rest in the subtle, during the daylight hours.

The intellect has classic "nice guy syndrome." It thinks that if it does what it deems to be virtuous deeds according to its own rules, it will be entitled to a specific return. It's great to be romantic, but it must be done properly. One must perform actions that support **everyone in the relationship**, and everyone is ultimately in relationship with everyone.

Work on your own purpose. Use your own *kuṇḍalinī*. Be the person that another would want to give their trust and time to. Someone fixated on personal gain is not ready for the cosmic ocean and the vast information and power it implies. Efforts are surrendered to the matriarch and gifts given by the matriarch. Sorry lads, that's it. You might never understand what she sees in you. You'll just have to trust and learn how to be in loving relationship with the world, the cosmic ocean, and the others.

Spiritual practices are played out in ordinary situations. How wonderful that people get married and have children and experience

[12] "Spiritual sacrifice is not about performing ceremonies, being a martyr to a cause, or affecting a pretence of spirituality. These things remove you from a natural, organic, playful life of innocent mischief. The true sacrifice is disrupting the addiction to materiality, and instead tending to the garden of visualisations, tones, and ideas. It is called sacrifice because there is a giving up of something that you hold close — your ingrained routines." Pryor. The Spirit of the Matter.

greater personal self-reflection. In close relationships people learn to manage energy and stoke the fire of devotion. The shared space of joy and pain with such raw intimacy creates a peak experience of empathy in ordinary life. Couples frequently know what the other is thinking. They mirror each other to build trust and they co-regulate to increase harmony. They worship one another's virtues, and modify themselves here and there to fit smoothly into the relationship container. This is natural, and it helps them approach life as a happy and productive team.

The mirroring (hopefully) goes smoothly, with each party somewhat conscious of the concessions and benefits, and finding ways to maintain healthy individual identity outside of the relationship. The mirroring **will also expose aspects** of each person which are so hardened they won't budge, and often are not recognised at all. Limiting beliefs so baked-in they evade self-examination. Kali reveals, via spontaneous response, aspects of self-image that have never been noticed and may appear terrifying when (often unintentionally) reflected back to you. Parents will relate to this from their children as well.

So we see that humanity already has spirituality built into it. There are ultimately no special texts or schools required. After all, people seem to be manifesting desires fairly reliably without yoga! But it is possible to work with greater intensity than the common path of mixed results and gradual development carried over to the next life. If you are holding this text right now, it may be the right tool at this moment.

A *yogi* is one who has decided to live in a specific manner based on the answer to the question, "what is the most fundamental thing?" This means living as the fully responsible consciousness who sculpts their projections in imagination and takes deliberate action, so that the world reflects their values and intention. As the Seer who sets the seen.

Everyone is courageous in their 20s, everyone can go all the way. As the years roll on and a few scars have accumulated, the influence of society creeps in and people often slide into stable normality. Life then involves interesting holidays, career development, socialising with friends, and learning how to raise children. All this with more or less struggle and variety compared to the neighbours.

People on the path of spirituality are at greater risk of a slip. They adopt the practices of spirituality and they collect the friends and decorations of the movement. They dive into the scene and live in vibrant and dynamic spontaneity. But as time passes it can become **routine spirituality** and **scheduled activities**. Years later, they still have occasional freaky experiences and share them with friends. They do the *yoga* classes and *kundalini* meditation and people acclaim their dedication. But has their self-image kept expanding to include even more of the subtle? Do they still hear the voice of the silence?

A *yogi* consistently ventures directly into the place of terrifying doubt and uncomfortable uncertainty until the intellect is bathed completely and permanently in the light. Yes, conventional life also includes plenty of challenge and elevation, but the *yogi* goes far into that until every last scrap of victimhood and separation has been cleaned up.

This is how the *yogi* attains *nirvikalpa* and merges with the Goddess.

What is Important

Śloka 42

पारमार्थिकजीवस्तु ब्रह्मइक्यं पारमार्थिकम्
प्रत्येति वीक्षते नान्यद्वीक्षते त्वनृतात्मना

pāramārthikajīvastu brahmikyaṃ pāramārthikam
pratyeti vīkṣate nānyad vīkṣate tvanṛtātmanā

The child of vision, the inner explorer, the naïve and fearless one knows himself as the Seer in the midst of strange forms and experiences. Vulnerability is constant awareness of the silent voice, even when the information given is gruelling.

Having identified our true feelings and desires, and having set a healthy self-image, we are ready to hear subtle insights. It is important to fully detach from the initial cravings. No more waiting or checking – find joy and purpose in the appreciation of everything and everyone else. There are parallel ventures that enrich the whole endeavour.

This attitude of abundance sounds lovely, and I believe it and always have. But some disagree and feel that scepticism is required to be a responsible adult. These are the sorts of introspections we do in our practice. We compare what **we say we believe** to how **we actually behave**. I write these words, but does a hidden part of me have doubt or negative belief? I am a good actor – have I fooled myself?

Lots of men have tough times, horrible childhoods and adulthoods. Some have it worse than others, and the lucky ones receive inspiration and skills from the process. We often come to appreciate the benefits received in amongst the trouble. But it can be hard to grasp (or admit) that the experience of disadvantaged men is akin to what all women experience. It is so easy to gloss over and thus perpetuate it.

Women are trained to be nice to men. When a man receives the benefit of a woman's company, has it ever been fairly earned? Has it been received on equal grounds? Not really. Girls are taught to always sacrifice, to "perform femininity", that beauty equals worthiness, and to never threaten a man's ego if they want to stay safe.

Relationships established through trauma-bonding can be a special case. When both parties are at rock bottom, there can be an unusual level of equality. Mutually degraded circumstances where both parties have been ravaged by global strife, bad families, class inequity etc. Even then, the man gets the benefit of a woman's conditioning to assist.

As discussed early in this book, life in a materialist culture is tainted by a focus on scarcity and limitation. The repercussions of monetisation are felt by everyone in their efforts to be free. Economic coercion is built into modern society, attenuating individuals' ability to live alone, to work fewer than 40 hours per week, to choose the most inspiring vocations possible. **But a far greater coercion** has been embedded much longer than neo-conservatism. Patriarchy and misogyny are the bedrock upon which civilisation rests. The sooner we all see it, the sooner we can make new choices.

What is the new choice? We cannot restore what we have never known. We simply have no clue what it would be like if there hadn't been thousands of years of patriarchy, and we would be fools to think we can tweak things from here to make it right.

Modern spirituality is often delusional, employing the classical materialist norms – but with a sprinkling of the supernatural on top. Similarly, anything we come up via the intellect in the gender equity space will be rooted in the thousand-year status-quo – with a sprinkling of gestures on top.

We can start again with the principles of *ahiṃsā* and *satya*, and the understanding that joyousness and the freedom to choose are the birthright of all. We can explore who we are really are, how we would like our world to look in each moment, and act from the combined entity of ego and subtle body.

It would be easy for me to keep banging the drum, to glibly encourage everyone to love themselves and move into a new earth where we all have equal access to energy and freedom and swim in the cosmic ocean. But I keep clicking my fingers and it doesn't change. Click, click. There is clearly still something to be done. There is a path, it can be as quick or slow as we each prefer. But it is one we must all navigate.

The only way that romance feels really good and authentic for me is when **I act as the masculine in devotion to the feminine**. Anything else feels fake. I have obvious physical, social, and economic power, and the natural expression must be upliftment of others. For me, this is the peak of romance, and it must go to the extent of sacrificing this body – or at least being willing to.

Just as Ramakrishna was ready to throw himself onto the sword of the giant statue of Kali, so too I am willing to die for love. *La belle dame sans merci*. Reconciliation of vast and ages-long injustice demands no less than this. **Take me now that we may be united forever**. As society progresses, the stance may soften or become less gender-specific, but it hasn't yet. There is a time and a place for savage poetic intent.

Of course, there is a tendency for men to try and make things right – on their own terms. The sentiment is appreciated, I'm sure, but the unilateral initiation of belated action to restore equal footing can be yet another violation. Men don't get to choose the form and timing. Indeed, the fury of a woman who is willing and able to be truthful and reflect the storms of her experience must be met with eternal willingness to fall at her feet. **To uplift we must be willing to be torn down**.

The fundamental action of restoration is to listen and speak as honestly as possible in every moment, to clean up the scraps of our local environment, our shared subtle sanctuary. Another is to enable fairness and time, to build material safety so that when desired, **if desired**, the full gamut of **stirring and unsafe** electricity can be enjoyed by all.

The Time We Waste

It is the time we waste for love that makes her so important.

Once, I had a $1000 coffee. It was extraordinary. I was at the airport, having arranged the perfect schedule of flights back to Australia. In all my travels this would be the most smooth and efficient return. During the brief stopover I wrote and sent my love a poem by voice note. I felt so incredibly light and joyous, having sweetly farewelled her. I was enjoying a coffee, looking at my phone, practicing the lines and sending them to her. It was a dream. The whole time the airport staff were trying to call me. I was looking at my phone but the calls did not come through. It meant $1000 for another flight and an extra 24 hours in Delhi, and it was perfect. It showed how meaningless is my attachment to efficiency compared to love's span across time and space. **I will always choose that sweet, wasteful lightness over illusory productivity.**

Men enjoy the love of women on unfair grounds. While this disparity exists, we might never be sure how much of her feelings are true, and how much comes from indoctrination, protection, and reputation. What an outrage. I don't want gradual improvement. The children of vision will start from scratch. Taking the whole content of this book and the idea of manifesting reality based on conviction and concentration, **what would you say if the magic genie granted you one wish?**

This question is famously difficult to answer without sliding to dullness with "I would wish for world peace" or "I would wish for a million dollars". We have talked about the struggle of the ego to reach beyond itself. We are offered a new earth if we can <u>even partially</u> define it in imagination. But the brain-in-a-skull, like Artificial Intelligence, struggles with truly original works.

So we ask the Goddess, and the answer she presents me is thus. Inequity between the experience of men and women in society is inextricably linked to the difficulty we have in completely unifying the ego with the subtle body, and becoming conscious creators. When we solve one, the other will be solved at the same time, and we will move on and around this earth in the ecstasy of unconditional love, playful positivity, and instant manifestation of everything we desire.

The Eyes of the Heart

Śloka 43 - 44

माधुर्यद्रवशैत्यानि नीरधर्मास्तरङ्गके
अनुगम्याथ तन्निष्ठे फेनेऽप्यनुगता यथा

mādhuryadravaśaityāni nīradharmāstaraṅgake
anugamyātha tanniṣṭe phene'pyanugatā yathā

साक्षिस्थास्सच्चिदानन्दा सम्बंधाद्व्यावहारिके
तद् द्वारेणानुगच्छंति तथैव प्रातिभासिके

sākṣisthāssaccidānandā sambaṃdhādvyāvahārike
tad dvāreṇānugacchaṃti tathaiva prātibhāsike

The feeling in *sat-cit-ānanda* is the master key. Sometimes outcomes appear orchestrated from a specific person, and at other times from varied currents of will. Increasingly, the *guru* takes the form of community, *la mort de l'auteur.* As with the source text named for *Śaṅkarā,* so too with this commentary. The conch shell is heard blowing and the Seer of all knows even imagination to be another manifested object.

Innovation comes from the subtle body and beyond. Creativity comes from non-verbal imagination when it is respected, frequently contacted, and made part of every waking moment. Visions commence when we open up the shining space.

Any state anticipated by the individual mind can be brought to the front and experienced as a physical reality. When actions are repeatedly made with that state in mind, it must come. If it appears immediately, great! If there is a delay, then we have reaped a dual benefit. We will enjoy it now in consciousness, and also begin elaborating the journey to its appearance. We may enjoy tangential excursions along the path since the outcome is assured.

When intention is held consistently high, things move quickly. Every shift can strike like lightning and the sequence of events can become rapidly ecstatic, bringing the same twitches as when falling asleep. It is best to be sitting in *padmāsana* at those times. However, the common tendency is to notice one shift, then quickly fall back into the name and form, waiting indefinitely for the next intentional moment.

Stay in *sat-cit-ānanda*! Remain aware of the space around and within you. Start with one minute, then two. Resist the urge to reach for your phone or to talk, even with yourself, about what you're experiencing. Hold your focus and hear the sound. The convulsions will stabilise, and you will live immersed in the Goddess. Feel satisfaction now, so that your circumstances can reformulate to match. Feel grateful now, and everything you desire will be drawn to you.

This method, this style of effort, is easily missed when we labour under the belief that we are just a brain with too much work on its plate.

I am infinite imagination, projecting forms and acting them out.

Take the liberty. It is not so serious. Change something and then change it back again. Learn to listen and interact with subtle forms. Magic is so easily missed in the rush to complete tasks. There is sparkling eye contact you subtly avoid, acts of kindness in the street that would take your breath away if truly observed for a moment.

Your willingness to validate, forgive, and accept everything you see, even scenes you find objectionable, is your power to re-project that energy according to preference. If you see a flash of an unpreferred choice, even when it seems horribly likely, validate it and remember who you are. Perhaps it **was** the likely outcome! Until you saw it just now and took the opportunity to gracefully recognise and re-affirm your preference. Name and form reconfigure according to your wishes, once they are brought in as valid and released from the grip of egoic attachment.

Appreciate that you are being asked what you want, that you are being offered choices. The rehearsal space of meditation encourages innovation and positive ideas to appear. Fear and hope are sparks to help us discover our preferences and beliefs. They are pure energy, mixed with old rules. The outcome is yours already. All that turmoil drew your attention, urged you to do what is required to **become who you really are, who you intend to be in this life**.

Do you harbour the belief that something else "out there" is better than this moment? What unique opportunity do you have right now?

Savour the seen and the unseen, rather than trying to measure or prove. Things pop up in their own good time, and there will always be a new desire to follow. Live in the joy of becoming, ***sukhino bhavantu.***

My favourite marigolds are flowering now and their passionfruit smell is delicious. Brush them lightly. Our desires are accents carried along the subtle and ever-present fragrance of the world.

There are messages your very own world would share with you.

The Complete Samādhi

Śloka 45 - 46

लये फेनस्य तद्धर्मा द्रवाद्यास्स्युस्तरङ्गके
तस्यापि विलये नीरे तिष्टंत्येते यथा पुरा

laye phenasya taddharmā dravādyāssyustaraṅgake
tasyāpi vilaye nīre tiṣṭaṃtyete yathā purā

प्रातिभासिकजीवस्य लये स्युर्व्यावहारिके
तल्लये सच्चिदानंदाः पर्यवस्यंति साक्षिणि

prātibhāsikajīvasya laye syurvyāvahārike
tallaye saccidānaṃdāḥ paryavasyaṃti sākṣiṇi

THE SEER SERVES without hesitation and perceives without resistance. The desires and projections of all individuals are instantly granted, in imagination first. Then, after a time, everything expressed becomes internalised once more. All of manifested reality can be understood in its source form. For every object, person, belief, desire, planet, and element an individual accepts, the multiverse knows itself a little more. Complete *samādhi* is infinite inclusivity and responsibility.

It was once stated that all human deaths are a suicide, that death is always chosen. The prevailing materialist worldview can't help but leave people in a state of fatigue and despair after decades of reducing themselves to fit in. There are traditions so entrenched that they seem morally right. The heartbreak of choosing between adventure and practicality, between feeding your family and helping another. Fights and manipulations to secure borders. Desires repeatedly squashed until people just want it to all be over.

It seems to make sense to plan your life using the intellect. It seems logical to start with protection and boundaries, before selecting the rest. But this is the snare, the fundamental error, and that primary decision over-rides all subsequent decisions.

When the sharply focused ego is in control, it cannot help but feel intimidated and isolated, and fear lures it into self-preservation.

But if the large and non-verbal subtle body is allowed to make the first move, she simply smiles, reflecting the expansive light of *brahman* for all to see. Ego glances over his shoulder, attracted by the shimmering, and chases her, like a dog chasing its tail. He realises he is in the presence of beauty incarnate, and partners with her for life, *le aspirants amoreaux*.

The devotion in life, the focus of our *bhakti*, must be beyond the physical, toward the attractive force, with a willingness to sacrifice that which is temporary. If the first decision is "no", the life story will be one of friction and the tendency to stay small.

You have always existed. Make your first decision "yes". Start with awareness of infinity. This life is temporary. **You are eternal**.

Just as the eyes are the instrument of the brain, this body and ego are the instruments of the larger You. You are the Seer, and you set the entire scene. When all is loved and embraced, you may express freedom in the spirit of a child asking innocent questions without filter.

Does the gazelle feel ecstasy as the lion sinks its teeth?

The freedom this *samādhi* brings is to re-formulate and re-express yourself all over again with innocence and play. The joy of upliftment and intentional action is relished, and setbacks become mere course corrections. Just as a sailor perceives the dark skies and the buffeting winds as a terrific boon, so too we see ghouls and traumas as lucky charms and naïve games.

You may consider yourself a weary old soul, ready to end this cycle of rebirth. But when sourness of mind is resolved and we enter *nirvikalpa samādhi*, frozen stiff as though bitten by a snake, what happens?

We return to source, to love of a flower who attracts and provokes, inspiring us to expand. Wide-eyed and grateful, we jump at the chance to start again this exploration of meaning. Clear and free, with all our conflict melted and re-shaped for the unconditional benefit of all.

"

I want to fathom her secrets;
I want her to come to me and say: "*I love you*,"
and if not that, if that is senseless insanity,
then... well, what is there to care about?
I am like one demented,
all I want is to be near her,
in the halo of her glory, in her radiance,
always, for ever, all my life.
I know nothing more!"

Fyodor Dostoyevsky, The Gambler
(edited)

Summary of the Techniques

1. **The Current Feeling**
   Śloka 24, *savikalpa samādhi* (on mood/object)

   a. **The truth of how you feel right now**. Happy, grumpy, some secret desire? Reveal your beliefs and appreciate their service.
   b. **What do you believe yourself to be**. Are you a brain in a human skull, a larger sphere of energy, the universe?
   c. **What is your personal self-image**. Regardless of the metaphysics, are you good, deserving, and trustworthy?

2. **The Desired Feeling**
   Śloka 25, *savikalpa samādhi* (on intention/vibration)

   a. **Write and affirm an evolving set of beliefs** relating to the three above and affirm them regularly.
   b. **All potential paths are true**, and your preference has been selected, now let it go, take it for granted.
   c. **Deepen allowance and trust,** savour all the excellent things in life, relinquish dialogue to remain expanded.
   d. **Live your life with a confidence** that seems delusional.

3. **Boundless Existence**
   Śloka 26, *nirvikalpa samādhi* (deliberate dissociation)

   a. **Regularly disarm the ego**, enter the non-physical space.
   b. **Expose the mind to the voice of the silence** so that the scraps of old beliefs are wiped and reset with the new.
   c. **Have a long-term perspective**, as though everything will come if you can leave it alone.
   d. **Beware the gradual slide** into scheduled spirituality, create art and theatre that rattles you, and perhaps others...

For worksheets and activities, visit **www.theseersetstheseen.com**.

www.ingramcontent.com/pod-product-compliance
Lightning Source LLC
Chambersburg PA
CBHW062042290426
44109CB00026B/2708
9780645121148